1

THE PRE-WAR BUSINESS CYCLE

1907 to 1914

STUDIES IN HISTORY, ECONOMICS AND PUBLIC LAW

EDITED BY THE FACULTY OF POLITICAL SCIENCE
OF COLUMBIA UNIVERSITY

Volume CVIII] [Number 1

Whole Number 243

THE PRE-WAR BUSINESS CYCLE

1907 to 1914

BY

WILLIAM CHARLES SCHLUTER

AMS PRESS
NEW YORK

COLUMBIA UNIVERSITY
STUDIES IN THE
SOCIAL SCIENCES

243

The Series was formerly known as
Studies in History, Economics and Public Law

Reprinted with the permission of Columbia University Press
From the edition of 1923, New York
First AMS EDITION published 1968
Manufactured in the United States of America

Library of Congress Catalogue Card Number: 68-57580

AMS PRESS, INC.
NEW YORK, N.Y. 10003

To

D. M. F.

PREFACE

THIS inquiry undertakes to determine the causes that produced the business depressions of 1910-11 and 1913 in the United States. Any such inquiry, however, involves also a discussion of the premature occurrence of those depressions as related to the normal ebb and flow of general business conditions abroad. It will be remembered that after the revival of 1909 was well under way, and a buoyant prosperity era was foreshadowed, the onward march of business progress continued uninterruptedly in Germany, England, and France—where only a mild reaction took place because of bad harvests—while in the United States there occurred the unexpected depression of 1910-11.

It will be remembered also that when the depression of 1913 occurred in the United States, universal business conditions were approaching the completion of a prosperity cycle, but that, even so, while business conditions in Europe were still prospering, this country sank into a state of depression.

The search for the causes of these depressions proceeds of necessity by the statistical method. But much of the statistical material used, reduced to a monthly basis, has not been embodied in this discussion because, in addition to being cumbersome, a great deal of it has been widely and systematically published elsewhere. We hope, therefore, to point conclusions from carefully chosen data concerning the factors conditioning business activity during 1907-14.

The specific problem of this treatise is the discovery of the causes of the business depressions of 1910-11 and 1913.

The last chapter, however, is devoted to an explanation of the varying lengths of business cycles, which we offer, based on the data and analyses in preceding chapters together with historical corroboration.

W. C. Schluter

CONTENTS

CHAPTER I

The Depression of 1908

CHAPTER II

The Revival of 1909

CHAPTER III

The Recurring Depression of 1910–11

PAGE

CHAPTER IV

Causes of the Depression of 1910–11

CHAPTER V

The Return of Prosperity in 1912

CHAPTER VI

The Depression of 1913

CHAPTER VII

The Causes of the Depression of 1913

PAGE

CHAPTER VIII

Varying Lengths of Cycles—Determining Factors

CHAPTER I

THE DEPRESSION OF 1908

Panic Conditions of 1907. For all modern nations that came under the sway of the capitalistic regime, the cumulative prosperity phase of the business cycle ended during the first half of 1907. The period of liquidation that followed ushered in the usual series of events characteristic of the transition of our modern business life from a period of prosperity to one of depression. The factors conditioning that process of liquidation began operating in the spring of that year, working cumulatively, gathering volume and momentum as the months went by. This cumulative progression produced such disruptions and dislocations in business relationships in Germany, France and England as to bring on a crisis, while in the United States the stresses engendered by the rapidity of the liquidation process upon our non-resilient credit system led to the panic of October, 1907.[1]

As early as January and February of 1907, the security market augured a recession of business activity in the United States. During those two months, prices of securities suffered a sharp decline, which in turn caused a complete demoralization of the market in March. Except for a short respite in mid-summer, when the market held, security prices continued on the down grade, until the panic in October. The decline in commodity prices began in the spring, when the demand for raw materials, especially cop-

[1] *Cf.* W. C. Mitchell, *Business Cycles*, p. 77.

per, began to slacken. This was followed by a drop in prices of manufactured articles during the month of October. In the meantime, the credit and investment market became more and more tense, developing a situation of severe and serious strain; whereas the physical volume of business continued strong and gave few signs of waning until November, when large industrial establishments and financial houses in New York began to fail, when bank failures occurred, and when practically all business relationships relaxed. These were the immediate causes of the panic, which led to a scramble for money and a general suspension of specie payment by the banks which, in the later months of 1907, availed themselves of every means of increasing the gold supply and other exchange media, in order to meet the exorbitant monetary demands. About the middle of December, a restoration of confidence, brought about by the importation of gold, and by various other means employed to increase the circulating medium, allayed somewhat the fears of the excited public, and bettered the situation.[1] Immediately following the closing weeks of 1907, business came to a standstill and the country passed into a period of depression, acute, but of short duration.[2]

Financial papers describe this depression of 1908 as one of the worst in the history of this country.[3] In Europe, also, although not so severe a period as it was in the United States, the year was one of depression from beginning to end.[4]

[1] The other means of payment provided included clearing-house loan certificates and deposit of the U. S. Treasury funds with banks, *cf. Quarterly Journal of Economics*, vol. xxii, p. 497, A. P. Andrew, "Substitutes for cash in panic of 1907." Total clearing-house loan certificates issued is here estimated at $334,000,000.

[2] *Ibid.*, p. 515.

[3] *Commercial and Financial Chronicle*, vol. lxxxix, pp. 5-15.

[4] *London Economist*, vol. lxviii, p. 155.

Business stagnation, it is necessary to observe, was most acute in industrial and trade circles.[1] The following statistics will indicate the degree of industrial inactivity in this country:

UNEMPLOYMENT

(DATA BY THE BUREAU OF STATISTICS OF THE STATE OF MASSACHUSETTS IN PER CENT ON BASIS OF 165,762 LABOR UNION MEMBERS IN THE STATE)

	1908	*1909*	*1910*	*1911*	*1912*	*1913*
March 31	17.9	11.4	7.1	10.4	14.1	11.3
June 30	14.4	6.4	7.0	6.6	5.3	6.4
Sept. 30	10.6	4.8	5.6	5.6	4.7	6.8
Dec. 31	13.9	9.4	10.2	9.7	9.1	10.4

(NUMBER OF UNEMPLOYED AMONG ORGANIZED WORKERS IN NEW YORK)[2]

	1907	*1908*	*1909*	*1910*	*1911*
March 31	77,270	138,131	74,543	62,811	96,608
Sept. 30	42,556	80,576	36,968	63,103	50,390

SALES, EXPENSES AND EARNINGS OF THE U. S. STEEL CORPORATION

(THIS CORPORATION CONTROLLED 60% OF THE FINISHED STEEL PRODUCTION IN 1908)

(*In million dollars*)

	1907	*1908*	*1909*
Gross sales	757	482	646
Total expenses	606	396	522
Net earnings	161	92	131

Early Revival in the Fnancial Market. Demoralization of the credit and investment market in the United States had become quite complete during the panic of 1907. The extreme demands upon the money and credit system, resulting from the abnormal liquidating process, caused such an acute decline in the value of securities and commodities, that no further downward revision of prices was possible.[3]

[1] *Mineral Industry*, vol. xvii, pp. 510-520.

[2] *N. Y. Department of Labor Bulletin*, no. 51, p. 103 and no. 49, p. 474.

[3] The rapid readjustment of business that occurs in conditions of panic, when the liquidation process becomes accentuated, seems to be

Proceeding then from a bed-rock level, as a result of this financial debacle, the course of investment enterprise tended optimistically upward; for any slight evidence of future increase in profits stimulated the security market to a state of buoyancy. In view of the collapse of security values in 1907, this recovery of the stock market was noteworthy, as may be seen by observing the comparative trend of security prices during the two years. The upward movement of prices of stocks and bonds was general.

A. RELATIVE PRICES OF 40 TRANSPORTATION STOCKS

(ADAPTED FROM MITCHELL'S BUSINESS CYCLES)

AVERAGE ACTUAL PRICES IN 1890–99 = 100

	1907		*1908*	
	Low	*High*	*Low*	*High*
January	243	270	163	186
February	234	252	150	169
March	193	243	158	182
December	158	176	240	264

B. RELATIVE PRICES OF 10 RAILROAD BONDS

AVERAGE ACTUAL PRICES IN 1890–99 = 100

	1907	*1908*
January	112.5	105.8
June	107.9	107.6
December	101.6	112.1

The volume of sales of securities increased to a remarkable degree:

more conducive to an earlier revival than where the liquidation process is gradual. Panic conditions precipitate a sudden fall in prices, to a degree often subnormal. Nevertheless, with such a sharp drop in prices, the price system becomes less deranged at the close of the period of liquidation than where the drop is gradual. On the other hand, if panic conditions are absent, and a slow and gradual process of liquidation occurs, the element of purposive restraint on the part of the banks and business enterprises leads to a great irregularity in price movements.

VOLUME OF SALES OF STOCKS AND BONDS ON THE NEW YORK EXCHANGE

	1907	1908
Stocks	*Number of shares (000 omitted)*	
January	22,703	16,595
July	12,811	18,881
December	12,636	23,002
Bonds	*Par value (000 omitted)*	
January	$45,308	$85,846
July	22,377	75,344
December	59,990	161,786

The pronounced growth of activity in the stock market during 1908 was comparable to that of the boom of 1904. The superabundance of loanable funds, the new rate increase for railroads, with the subsequent rise in their earnings, all gave impetus to speculation for higher prices. Slight flurries occurred in the stock market in February, brought about by Roosevelt's letter to the Interstate Commerce Commission concerning the reduction of wages of railroad employees, and as a result of the disquieting political situation in Eastern Europe over the German-French Moroccan controversy. Although a decline in steel prices and general divided reductions produced some irregularity in the price movement of securities during June, nevertheless specialty stocks consistently continued to advance in price, and copper mining and industrial shares figured strongly in the rise of the latter part of the summer. Success attended a large flotation of bonds. In the fall, the recurrence of trouble in the Balkans precipitated selling upon foreign account.

European Security Markets. During 1908, improvement in the European security markets was far less energetic than it was in the United States, being confined to a mild recurrence of activity during the latter part of the year.[1]

[1] *Volkswirtschaftliche Chronik*, 1908, p. 856. It is here alleged that

In Germany the inactivity of the bourse was reflected in the low yield of taxes on securities, (Effektenstempel) and on bourse sales. Although the volume of business was not great, prices of stocks advanced somewhat after the month of May, while because of the large number of new bond issues in 1908, especially government loans bond prices remained depressed and, later, declined still further. Their market value was also influenced by the effort of the Reichsbank, during the greater part of the year, to attract gold by maintaining high discount rates.

The conditions prevailing in the German security market are well illustrated by the figures given below:

A. Yield of Taxes on Sales on German Bourses and Taxes on Securities

(in thousands of dollars)

	Taxes on Sales	*Taxes on Securities*
1907	$2,625	$8,557
1908	2,537	5,827
1909	4,700	8,805

B. The Average Price in Marks, of all Interest-bearing and Dividend-yielding Securities Dealt in on the Berlin Bourse, as Computed by the Volkswirtschaftliche Chronik

1907	*Interest-bearing*	*Dividend-yielding*
January	93.22	160.59
April	91.48	151.76
August	89.27	145.21
November	89.93	143.05
Yearly average	90.79	149.29
1908		
January	91.24	144.44
April	90.22	145.29
August	90.96	146.56
November	91.19	147.62
Yearly average	90.96	145.34

the dearth of capital in Europe at the beginning of 1908 and the reaction caused by the American panic retarded speculation there, but it was more likely the result of the gradual and prolonged process of liquidation in Europe.

C. ADMISSION OF SECURITIES ON GERMAN BOURSES
(PAR VALUE IN MILLION DOLLARS)

	Total	*Government (Imperial, State and Municipal)*
1907	$613	$270
1908	923	551
1909	835	394

The London stock market remained relatively inactive throughout the greater part of the year 1908. The severe industrial and trade depression in this country, famine and crop failure in India, critical times in Egypt, and domestic labor difficulties, especially in the cotton and ship industries, combined to produce this inactivity. In spite of this, prices of securities advanced somewhat. The *London Bankers Magazine* reported an increase of 3.9 per cent in the average price of 387 securities. Among these, American railway stocks and bonds, and American copper shares, figured prominently, while industrial shares, generally, remained static, and bonds continued weak. Security prices on the Paris bourse advanced, even though the market continued in a state of nervousness and developed little strength. Advances were limited prinicipally, however, to the Rentes and railroad bonds. The *Economiste Européen* shows in its computation of the price of 163 securities upon the Paris bourse that, although the volume of sales did not increase, the average price rose 2.17 per cent during the year as against a loss of 0.86 per cent in 1907 and 3.52 per cent in 1906. The chief impetus to the activity of 1908 on European bourses was given by the strong speculative advances in prices of securities in the United States.

Readjustments in the Money Market. The excessive interest rates, occasioned by the panic of 1907 in the United States, left their impress on the foreign, as well as on the domestic money market, which did not come to rest until the spring months of 1908. While rates in the four important money markets of the world underwent a general readjustment up to the month of July, those in the American and German markets (with the exception of call-loan rates in New York which continued extremely low), retained a higher level than were maintained in the French and English markets.

RATES OF INTEREST UPON THE MONEY MARKETS OF UNITED STATES, GERMANY, ENGLAND AND FRANCE

	United States				Germany			
	1907		1908		1907		1908	
	Call rate %	60–90 day rate %	Call rate %	60–90 day rate %	Bank rate %	Market rate %	Bank rate %	Market rate %
January	6.15	6.15	6.59	4.75	6.50	4.50	6.66	4.98
February	4.38	5.94	1.81	5.06	6.00	4.68	6.00	4.48
March	6.38	6.19	1.85	5.63	6.00	5.40	5.75	4.40
April	2.35	5.92	1.72	4.38	6.00	4.65	5.25	4.11
May	*2.31* [2]	*5.40* [2]	1.66	3.94	5.75	*4.44* [2]	5.00	3.91
June	3.13	5.50	1.52	*3.69* [2]	*5.50* [2]	4.66	4.50	3.33
July	4.55	5.75	*1.22* [2]	3.75	5.50	4.44	*4.00* [2]	*2.76* [2]
December	14.65	8.00 [1]	2.90	3.85	7.25	7.07	4.00	2.92

	England				France			
	1907		1908		1907		1908	
	Bank rate %	Market rate %	Bank rate %	Market rate %	Bank rate %	Market rate %	Bank rate %	Market rate %
January	5.40	4.82	5.00	4.18	*3.00* [2]	3.00	4.00	3.41
February	5.00	4.73	4.00	3.33	3.00	*2.91* [2]	3.25	2.68
March	5.00	5.01	3.25	2.81	3.25	3.05	*3.00* [2]	2.61
April	3.50	3.64	3.00	2.57	3.50	3.38	3.00	2.75
May	*4.00* [2]	*3.22* [2]	3.87	1.98	3.50	3.39	3.00	2.36
June	4.00	3.78	*2.50* [2]	1.34	3.50	3.44	3.00	1.86
July	4.00	3.56	2.50	*1.26* [2]	3.50	3.34	3.00	*1.59* [2]
December	7.00	5.90	2.50	1.41	4.00	4.00	3.00	2.33

[1] nominal.

[2] lowest.

After the readjustment of interest rates upon a lower level, a world-wide ease reigned in the money market, since business depression was universal. Gold exports from New York were heavy from April to July, because of the low interest rates on call money, and yet loanable funds remained ample for all purposes, and in the New York market there was not the slightest flurry after the latter part of January, not even after stock speculation had again made progress. In June the surplus reserves of the New York Clearing House banks reached $68,233,025, the highest figure in fourteen years. On account of the industrial stagnation that prevailed, money remained plentiful and credit was cheap, and this in spite of extraordinary inroads upon the world's money supply. The United States Treasury, because of decreasing receipts, recalled large quotas of funds from the banks, with the result that government deposits in banks stood at only $121,431,154 on December 30, 1908, as against $256,920,155 in January 1, 1908.[1] State banks of New York being required by law to increase their reserves, those state banks outside of the clearing-house association increased their money holdings from $49,000,000 on February 8, 1908, to $108,400,000 on December 26, 1908.

The significant features of conditions in the European money markets were threefold: first, the urgent government demand for capital; second, the attempt of continental banks to increase their gold holdings, and, third, the homeward flow of foreign invested capital as a result of the relaxation in requirements for funds, due to the general business depression. The Reichsbank maintained higher discount rates for the greater part of 1908, in order to attract gold, and to influence a rapid absorption of govern-

[1] *U. S. Treasury Report*, 1908, pp. 16 *et seq.*

ment loans. The Bank of France made an astonishing increase in its gold reserves. This increase was made possible mainly because of the great return flow of capital to France in the form of gold, the widespread business depression having made borrowing unnecessary for countries dependent upon foreign capital. Additions to the gold reserve of the Reichsbank for the year netted $63,265,800, while that of the Bank of France increased $155,731, 200. The principal Continental banks increased their gold reserves $265,914,012. This is significant, as will be pointed out later, in spite of the fact that such an accretion to the gold reserve might be expected to occur in the midst of a business depression. The greater part of this gold came from North America, Australia, and England, in many cases where exchange rates did not warrant the gold movement.

Among the European nations, England suffered most from the depression, as many industries were completely stagnant and unemployment was great. The position of England offers a contrast to that of the Continental European countries, with reference to gold movements. Money rates were relatively low in comparison with those of other European countries, and the Bank of England lost part of its gold reserve.[1] A striking feature of the gold movement was the failure of a large part of the supply to pass through the London market in 1908. During the summer the international money market became settled, and low interest rates prevailed, in spite of a slight degree of unrest in the fall due to the political disturbances in Southeastern Europe.

Movements of Commodity Prices. Initiated in the

[1] Whether there lies, back of this outflow of funds, a hidden policy, is a mere conjecture; however, because of England's peculiar dependency upon foreign trade, it may be seen that this flow of funds and gold to foreign fields would react upon the domestic industries by aiding the revival of foreign markets.

spring and summer of 1907, the movement of commodity prices continued downward in the United States, and came to a halt in the middle of 1908. General wholesale prices reached their lowest point in July and August, 1908, subsequently, recovery was marked. The United States Bureau of Labor Statistics has computed the index number of wholesale prices with the following results:[1]

AVERAGE ACTUAL PRICES 1890-99 = 100

	Commodities 1907				*Commodities 1908*			
	All	*Raw*	*Mfgd.*	*Farm*	*All*	*Raw*	*Mfgd.*	*Farm*
January	127.9	134.7	126.3	129.0	125.7	124.3	126.1	129.8
February	129.0	136.1	127.3	134.6	124.4	123.9	124.7	*128.8* [b]
April	129.1	133.9	128.0	136.5	124.0	124.0	124.0	134.2
May	129.6	136.0	128.0	139.9	122.4	*122.4* [b]	122.4	135.0
June	130.1	*136.9* [a]	128.5	144.2	121.5	123.8	121.1	132.8
July	130.3	134.2	129.4	140.5	121.7	124.8	120.9	134.0
August	130.2	132.3	129.7	141.0	*121.4* [b]	125.3	*120.5* [b]	133.8
September	130.8	132.8	*130.3* [a]	*145.4* [a]	121.8	125.6	120.9	132.7
October	*131.0* [a]	134.3	130.2	144.4	122.1	127.1	120.9	133.9
December	126.4	124.2	127.0	128.3	123.6	132.2	121.5	135.2

[a] *Highest.* [b] *Lowest.*

From the above table the characteristics of comparative trends in price movements of separate commodities become evident. Those of raw materials reached bottom in May, 1908, and those of manufactured articles in August, 1908, and while the former made sharp advances during the remaining part of the year, the latter lingered along a low level until December, when a sharp advance occurred. Again, the prices of farm products remained unresponsive to the general price movement of other commodities. After

[1] The U. S. Bureau of Labor's list of 15 articles manifested a sharp seasonal influence in the retail price index number. The index number rises sharply from May, 1907 to January, 1908, then declines to May and subsequently indicates a sharp recovery similar to the previous year. The trend on the whole was upward. *Cf. infra*, p. 25.

a sudden rise in the first two months of the year, occasioned by the small harvests of 1907, prices of farm products fluctuated on one general level until December. This was caused by the somewhat moderate yield of 1908, which was, however, sufficient to meet the existing demand during a period of contracted purchasing power, affecting both consumers and producers. Subsequently, a sharp upward movement set in, parallel with the same movement in manufactured articles.

A detailed study of some of the commodity markets discloses some interesting features. Prices of steel products, under the influence of the U. S. Steel Corporation, whose policy was to maintain prices in the face of a general decline, were "stepped down" on two occasions during the year, namely in June and in July, as shown below:

Actual Prices of Steel Products at Pittsburgh

1908	*Steel billets* (*$ per gross ton*)	*Wire nails* (*c. per lb.*)	*Beams and tank plates* (*c. per lb.*)	*Soft bars* (*c. per lb.*)
January	28.00	.0205	.0170	.0160
May	28.00	.0205	.0170	.0160
June	*25.75*	*.0197*	*.0162*	*.0145*
July	*25.00*	*.0195*	*.0160*	*.0140*
December	25.00	.0195	.0160	0140

The price of coal underwent little change throughout the year. Pittsburgh prices remained $1.15 for mine-run coal at the mine for both rail and river shipment. Copper prices, laboring under the influence of a huge overstock, together with speculation on future demand, averaged 13.2 cents per lb. for electrolytic at New York, as against 20.0 cents in 1907.

A perusal of European price statistics for 1908 indicates a recession of commodity prices similar to that which occurred in the United States. One qualification, however, should be noted, namely, that the price fluctuation confined itself within narrower limits than it did in this country.[1] The increased cost of living, resulting from the rise in retail prices, was the cause of universal complaint. In Germany, France, and England retail food prices were still high, while wholesale prices declined. A retail price index number is available only for England.

RETAIL PRICE INDEX NUMBER FROM THE UNITED STATES BUREAU OF LABOR

15 COMMODITIES—1913 = 100

	1907	*1908*
January	83.c	85.6
March	81.1	83.1
May	79.8	81.8
July	80.8	83.4
September	82.2	84.3
November	84.5	87.2
Average for yr.	81.9	84.2

RETAIL PRICE INDEX NUMBER FOR ENGLAND FROM THE BOARD OF TRADE LABOR GAZETTE

WEIGHTED FOR 23 ARTICLES—1900 = 100

1905	102.8
1906	102.0
1907	105.0
1908	107.5
1909	107.6

[1] Index number of wholesale prices from the London *Economist*:

	1907	*1908*	*1909*
January	2.494	2.309	2.196
May	2.601	2.188	2.225
September	2.457	2.200	2.258
November	2.360	2.198	2.333

Monthly index numbers of prices are not available for Germany and France, but the yearly figures indicate a recession comparable to the one here quoted. Index numbers for these two countries show a decline in prices of about 9% for 1908.

Changes in Volume of Production and Trade. Production and trade experienced a universal reaction during the year. Because of diminishing purchasing power and disruption of business relationships, over-production became quite general. Statistics indicate a standstill in some industries, and a decline in many. Although conditions were bad enough in England, the United States, as usual, suffered most. The acute recession of prices, the sudden contraction of great volumes of industrial activity and consumption in this country,—these found their echo throughout Europe and were reflected in markets generally. Had the contraction of business been less violent, and the depressing factors less extraordinary here, Europe, and especially England, would have been better equipped to moderate the consequent state of depression there.

In the United States the physical volume of business remained small until the fall of the year, as indicated by bank clearings outside of New York. Earnings of railroads, also, show a contraction of production and trade.[1] Imports contracted considerably in January and remained small in volume until fall. Exports continued strong the first three months of the year, but later, declined sharply. The tables presented below indicate the general decline in the volume of business during 1908:

BANK CLEARINGS IN THE UNITED STATES

(IN BILLIONS OF DOLLARS)

	Total	*Outside of New York*	*Stewart's index number of production*
1907	$145,176	$57,994	89
1908	132,272	52,996	84
1909	165,838	62,249	94

[1] In December railroad earnings became somewhat faulty as an index of the volume of business, because of a 10 per cent increase in rates.

Imports and Exports of Foodstuffs, Raw Materials and Manufactured Products of United States [1]

(adapted from Mitchell's computation)

relative figures 1890-99 = 100

	Imports			Exports		
	Foodstuffs	Raw materials	Manufactured	Foodstuffs	Raw materials	Manufactured
07	118	257	210	122	207	307
08	112	196	174	124	194	311
09	126	243	171	104	182	278

Figures showing the volume of business done in particular industries are indicative of the extent of the contraction in production as a whole. The coal trade, in general, showed a falling off of from 20 to 25 per cent in 1908. Anthracite fields were affected less than bituminous. Few producers engaged in any general price cutting, for they felt that it would not be a means of bringing more business. Some small producers lowered prices, but with no appreciable effect upon the demand.[2] In the copper industry overproduction prevailed. The smelters had already severely curtailed production as early as October, 1907, and by the beginning of the year 1908 an unsold stock of 120,000,000 lbs. of refined copper was being held in the domestic market. There was a fairly active export trade in copper, but the industry was subject to long periods of dullness, interspersed with fitful spurts of activity when certain immense quantities of surplus copper were unloaded by way of speculation. By the end of 1908, 122,357,266 lbs. of copper remained on hand. The iron and steel industries met sharp reverses in

[1] If the monthly figures are examined, it will be noted that the increases in exports of foodstuffs and manufactured products in 1908 were the result of efforts in the later months of the year, to find foreign markets for overstocks of foodstuffs, and in the earlier months for overstocks in manufactured products.

[2] *Mineral Industry*, vol. xvii, p. 165.

the latter part of 1907, these continuing until the middle of 1908, when price reductions stimulated a weak demand that increased production only a trifle, (as indicated by the statistics of pig iron production, and those showing the unfilled order of the U. S. Steel Corporation.) [2] The sharp and rapid curtailment of production at the close of 1907 reduced the production capacity of steel concerns to 40 per cent, a basis lower than any that had prevailed for eight years. In addition to this, the U. S. Steel Corporation adopted a policy of control which produced conditions in the iron and steel trades unprecedented in previous depressions. This corporation adroitly used its domination of the steel industry by combining with certain large independents, thereby succeeding in holding the industry to a policy of maintaining prices in the face of a lessening demand.[1] With the exception of a few small reductions, which in no way affected business, this defiant attitude continued throughout the year. The pig iron industry remained an open market during 1908, but it too labored under the restricting influence of the price policy of the steel concerns. Consumers generally were well aware of the wide margin arbitrarily maintained between quotations of pig iron and finished steel products, and this recognition provoked abstinence from buying. Unquestionably, some contraction of the iron and steel industry was normally to be expected, because of the widespread business depresison, but that the price-maintenance policy further retarded production is equally certain, though to what extent it would be difficult to say.

The physical volume of business in this country was somewhat augmented in the fall by a good crop yield. Corn and cotton harvests were very favorable, and while wheat

[1] *Ibid.*, p. 512.

[2] *Cf. ibid.*, p. 510. Also *Chronicle*, vol. lxxxix, p. 6.

fell a little below expectations, the yield was not subnormal. In comparison with this state of affairs in America, crops in other countries were only moderate in yield. Corn production in Europe was under normal, and in Russia, as in France, the wheat crop was particularly meagre. These countries therefore failed to feel this impetus to business.

In Germany the depression in industry and trade increased markedly during the summer and autumn. Iron remained depressed, and the pig-iron market was so demoralized that it caused the dissolution of the pig-iron syndicate. The textile industry showed sporadic signs of recuperation during the second half of the year. The coal situation was least unfavorably affected.[1] Foreign commerce declined, imports showing the contraction more than exports. Just as raw materials among imports decreased most markedly, so, among exports, manufactured articles showed the greatest falling off,—a further indication of the industrial inactivity that prevailed. France, in a milder degree, gave evidence of a similar recession in production and trade. Imports of all commodities figured in the decline, while the greatest decrease in exports occurred in raw materials and manufactured goods. Trade contracted especially with the United States. It must be noted, however, that France's volume of domestic business suffered no decline. If the industrial depression and the unemployment situation were severe upon the continent, they were worse in England. As in Germany, the diminished volume of England's foreign trade was characterized by a decrease in imports of raw materials, and a corresponding decrease in the export of manufactured articles. England's foreign markets moreover were adversely affected by the universal depression. In addition, famine and bad harvests in India, and difficulties in Egypt added their weight to the prevailing

[1] *Volkswirtschaftliche Chronik*, 1908, pp. 808 *et seq.*

depression, especially in the textile trades. The degree of industrial inactivity reached in European countries can be judged by a perusal of the comparative statistics relating to unemployment, as quoted in the following chapter.[1] Meantime, a study of the comparative indexes of volume of business in Germany, France, and England, would prove instructive.

(IN MILLIONS OF DOLLARS)

	Germany			*France*			*England*		
	1907	*1908*	*1909*	*1907*	*1908*	*1909*	*1907*	*1908*	*1909*
Gross railroad earnings	$653	$642	$677	$328	$335	$344	$546	$538	$539
Bank clearings.	10,800	10,900	12,300	5,000	5,200	5,700	62,000	59,000	65,800
Imports	2,082	1,824	2,028	1,201	1,089	1,205	2,696	2,498	2,595
Exports	1,629	1,522	1,569	1,080	975	1,104	2,073	1,835	1,840

Investment and Credit Conditions. The high money rates, inherited from the panic of 1907, continued during the first three or four months of 1908. They were followed, as has been seen, by a universal ease of money rates which exerted a propitious influence upon the investment markets. In the United States, financial enterprise centered

LOANS AND DISCOUNTS OF NEW YORK CLEARING HOUSE BANKS AND ALL NATIONAL BANKS

(IN MILLIONS OF DOLLARS)

	All national banks		*New York clearing house banks*	
January	$4,505	——	$1,069	$1,129
February	——	$4,452	1,088	1,147
March	4,573	——	1,056	1,163
May	4,664	4,551	1,131	1,208
July	——	4,640	1,115	1,266
September	——	4,782	1,093	1,311
December	4,623	4,879	1,169	1,320

Compare with the volume of security sales above, page 17.

[1] *Cf. infra*, p. 48.

its activity in the security market, where funds were in demand. This is corroborated by the rapid expansion of loans and discounts in the New York clearing house banks, an expansion corresponding to the increasing volume of sales, and the rising prices of securities. (Banks in the interior were later in augmenting their loans.) Flotations of new securities, evidenced by listings of new issues on the New York stock exchange, increased markedly. New issues of industrial stocks diminished, while bond issues increased, rapidly, especially in railroads. Building operations were everywhere in abeyance during the first quarter of the year of 1908, but increased sharply thereafter. Statistical estimates of the new security issues and building operations are listed below:

LISTINGS OF NEW SECURITIES UPON THE NEW YORK STOCK EXCHANGE

(IN MILLION DOLLARS)

	Bonds	*Stocks*
1907	$247	$159
1908	649	124
1909	713	297

MONTHLY VALUES OF BUILDING PERMITS ISSUED FOR TWENTY LEADING CITIES

(IN HUNDRED THOUSAND DOLLARS)

	1907	*1908*	*1909*
1st quarter	$1,199	$ 607	$1,403
2nd quarter	1,860	1,241	1,997
3rd quarter	1,179	1,125	1,583
4th quarter	826	1,260	1,171
Total	$5,064	$4,233	$6,154

(Adapted from the *Harvard Review of Economic Statistics.*)

In Europe, contrary to the situation of this country, the contraction of bank loans continued throughout 1908:

COMMERCIAL AND COLLATERAL LOANS OF THE REICHSBANK, BANK OF FRANCE AND JOINT STOCK BANKS OF ENGLAND AND WALES

(IN MILLION DOLLARS)

	Joint Stock Banks		*Reichsbank*		*Bank of France*	
	1907	*1908*	*1907*	*1908*	*1907*	*1908*
January	——	——	$259	$299	$373	$360
May	$2,071	$2,098	264	251	323	282
November	2,140	2,077	322	216	351	242

The balances of the German Joint Stock Banks show an increase in discounts of $2,316,000 in 1908 over those of 1907, while the item of "Advances and Contangoes" increased $62,938,000 over that of the previous year. This increase can be traced directly to the credit requirements of the large new bond issues, principally governmental.

The reason for the contraction in the use of bank credit is to be found probably in the fact that the European security market remained relatively inactive as compared with the security market in the United States; and that the European commodity markets continued in a state of liquidation practically throughout the year. On the other hand, however, there was in Europe a strong demand for investment capital.

NEW ISSUES OF SECURITIES IN GERMANY, FRANCE AND ENGLAND

(IN MILLION DOLLARS)

	England	*Germany*	*France*
1907	$593	$480	$569
1908	935	795	698
1909	887	770	842

The volume of government securities bulked large in the bond totals, closely followed by railroad obligations; whereas stock issues were small.—except in France, where they gained over that of the previous year.[1]

[1] It must be noted that from 40% to 50% of issues in France and Germany in 1908 were government bonds. The same is partially true for England, where issues were, however, largely foreign and colonial; railroad bonds, especially were issued in great volume. *Cf. Volkswirtschaftliche Chronik*, 1908, pp. 913-14.

Commercial Failures. The process of purging the industrial organization of weak and inefficient business concerns was notably active during the year of 1908, in all countries. The largest number of failures occurred in Germany, where they increased from 9,860 in 1907 to 11,570 in 1908. In England these failures increased during the same period from 4,111 to 4,306, and in France from 8,106 to 8,159. In the United States, also, the number of commercial failures, as reported by Bradstreets, increased from 10,285 in 1907 to 14,066 in 1908. Failures were greater in number during the early part of 1908 and grew gradually less as the year went on.

Political Factors. The political situation in the United States acquired its character from the presidential campaign then in progress. Since the success of the Republican Party was pretty much taken for granted by the business world generally, the assumption that higher tariff rates would be inaugurated stimulated business activity. The issues concerning trust legislation evidently gave rise to no depressing influences. The Interstate Commerce Commission, although granting some rate increases, prohibited many rate advances. In addition, the 2-cent per mile passenger fare was generally put into practice.

In Europe the political situation became somewhat disquieting in the fall. Germany and France entered into a controversy over the Casablanca affair, while trouble also developed in the Balkans. In addition there occurred many local political disturbances in India, Persia, Egypt, Morocco, Portugal and Venezuela. The influences of these political factors accentuated liquidation in the European money markets, especially, in international loans. However, no far-reaching effects were noticeable, for the industrial situation was largely under the influence of the economic forces of liquidation and business readjustment.

Conclusion. During the greater part of 1908, forces making for business readjustment were vigorously at work. The actual process of liquidation and state of depression were confined to the first half of the year, during which time, as has been seen, inactivity in production and trade were most pronounced. But by spring, the large number of commercial failures had grown less. The increase in supply of loanable funds, caused by increased bank reserves, brought about an extraordinary cheapness of credit, which led to an expansion of loans in New York.[1] Prices of raw materials and farm products had ceased to decline. Evidences were manifold that readjustment was taking place upon a lower level of costs to meet the downward revision of prices. By the fall of the year bank loans in the interior began to expand, prices of manufactured articles swung upward, a large number of new securities were issued containing a large proportion of railroad bonds, and the security market generally drew breath and began to revive.

European business conditions, during 1908, gave evidence of similar changes, but in a more moderate degree. A milder spirit of speculation animated the European security markets; larger volumes of new securities were issued, mainly governmental obligations; continental countries, far from feeling a plenitude of money, engaged in a scramble for gold; commodity prices receded continuously, giving evidence of a much more gradual process of liquidation than that which took place in the United States.

[1] The loans of the New York Clearing House banks began to increase in the spring, with the revival of the security market and the heavy issue of new securities.

CHAPTER II

The Revival of 1909

The Nature of the Revival. As seen in the previous chapter, evidences of revival in industrial and trade circles in the United States became noticeable in the fall of 1908.[1] Speculation in the cotton and copper trades was noticeable even during the summer months, but the actual revival came in the fall, and the immediate circumstances that stimulated it are to be found in the favorable crop estimate and good yields marketed at remunerative prices; the increased, earnings of the railroads; the heavy use of investment funds especially those secured by large issues of bonds procured at low rates of interest; and the demand for goods arising out of the depletion of stocks—this demand for producers' and consumers' goods was fostered by an increase in purchasing power.[2] Following is a table indicative of the favorable conditions in the agricultural and railroad industries:

Crop Yields and Prices in the United States During 1908

	Cotton		*Corn*		*Wheat*	
	Bales	*Cents per lb.*	*Million bushels*	*Cents per bu.*	*Million bushels*	*Cents per bu.*
1907	11,107,179		2,592		634	
Jan.		11.30		.42		.73
July		10.70		.54		.98
Dec.		9.10		.59		1.02

[1] *Cf.* W. C. Mitchell, *op. cit.*, p. 83; also *Chronicle*, vol. lxxxix, p. 10.

[2] *Cf. supra*, p. 31.

1908	13,241,799		2,669		665	
May		11.50		.75		1.05
Aug.		10.85		.79		.93
Oct.		9.45		.73		1.03
Nov.		9.55		.64		1.05
Dec.		9.35		.59		1.03
1909	10,004,949		2,552		737	
Jan.		9.25		.60		1.06
July		12.20		.71		1.23
Dec.		14.65		.64		1.17

Corn and wheat prices at Chicago.
Cotton prices at New York.

TREND OF RAILROAD NET EARNINGS—BRADSTREETS

INCREASE (+) AND DECREASE (—) IN PER CENT OVER PREVIOUS MONTH

	1908
January	—27.4
May	—25.1
August	—10.3
October	+ 6.3
November	+12.2
December	+20.8

For employment statistics *cf. supra*, p. 15.

In comparison with the incipient revival of this country, the inert condition of European industry and trade at the close of 1908 stands out in sharp contrast. There, harvest yields were only moderate, and unemployment increased throughout the year. The unsettled political situation, too, produced by the Balkan controversy and the Franco-German dispute over the Moroccan question, left its impress upon business conditions. So far reaching were these influences that the business revival in Europe was delayed until the first few months of 1909 had passed.

The Security Markets. The New York stock market showed the influence of the industrial and trade revival in a rise in prices and an increasing volume of sales during the first nine months of 1909, but the general upward trend came to a halt in September, and during the later months of the year a decline set in which affected a great many securities.

RELATIVE PRICES OF 40 RAILROAD STOCKS AND 10 RAILROAD BONDS
adapted from Mitchell's *Business Cycles*
and
AVERAGE PRICES OF 12 INDUSTRIAL AND 20 RAILROAD STOCKS
as given by the *Wall Street Journal*

1909	*40 railroad stocks*		*20 railroad stocks*	*12 industrial stocks*	*10 railroad bonds*
	Low	*High*			
January	247	271	118.9	85.6	113.2
March	248	267	118.7	83.9	113.6
May	270	286	124.8	90.9	113.6
July	274	288	129.4	94.8	113.0
August	274	296	131.6	97.8	112.9
September	272	292	130.0	98.0	112.2
November	279	298	128.0	98.2	111.2
December	284	307	128.0	98.0	111.2

VOLUME OF STOCK AND BOND SALES ON NEW YORK STOCK EXCHANGE

1909	*Stocks—No. of shares* (000 omitted)	*Bonds—par value* (000 omitted)
January	17,276	$134,867
March	13,651	80,286
May	16,495	114,760
July	12,807	91,745
September	19.982	88,933
November	18,770	84,711

The movement was not, however, synchronous for all securities. Though prices of industrials culminated in September, those of better grade railroad stocks continued upward until the end of December. Bonds, in contrast, owing to rising interest rates and large new issues, declined in price and volume of sales continuously throughout the year. The only marked weakness in the general movement displayed during these first nine months occurred in February and March, when standard stocks fluctuated within narrow limits and low grade stocks varied over a rather wide range. This growing weakness is to be attributed to the wild price-cutting that took place in the steel and copper industries. When the determined policy of the leading steel interests, to maintain prices in spite of general reductions, was finally broken in March, the halting and hesitation of the iron and steel markets disappeared, competition was once more possible, and steel prices underwent a sympathetic revision in accordance with the general lowering price level. Concident with these happenings in the security market, American securities were sold in considerable quantities by London during February and March, and so a large amount of European capital was withdrawn from this country. In August, Mr. Harriman's failing health exerted a depressing effect upon the value of Union Pacific Railroad securities, and caused another slight disturbance on the stock exchange. While stocks continued to rise during the summer and early fall, the selling of American securities held by foreign countries became more and more noticeable. In June, a plan to sell steel stocks in Paris failed to materialize, and this failure produced a slight reaction upon the security market here. Indeed, there was a decided apathy of foreign investors toward American securities generally, the reluctance of the French investor being especially marked. Favorable influences remained, however,—namely, the excellent condition prevailing in the transportation business, rising commodity prices, and growing profits in industry. But by September, as previously stated, the peak had been reached and depressing influences began to operate. Because money became dearer both in Europe and in the United States, American securities were sold on foreign account in greater proportions, and European investment markets hesitated to absorb American borrowings. Domestic occurrences, too, exerted a depressing influence,—the Standard Oil decision, for instance; the pronouncement of the illegality of the prospective copper combine; the heavy issues of New York Central stocks, with the announcement of other new railroad issues; and the large volume of listings upon the stock exchange during the year. All these factors, in conjunction with the higher rates of interest in the fall, combined to check the rapid advance of security prices in September.

It must be noted that most of the European bourses experienced a similar halt in advances, during September and October, which appears to have been a sympathetic reflection of the untoward conditions mentioned above as having developed in the security market in the Unted States. In Germany, the whole year was one of gradually increasing responses to many stimulating influences, beginning in the early months with a greater activity in bonds, and progressing, toward spring, to a veritable state of animation, as the result of the decided revival in the United States, of the abundance of funds, active speculation in colonial securities, and finally, the revival of production and trade within Germany itself. In spite of slight reactions in May, June and October, the average prices of bonds, as figured by the *Volkswirthschaftliche Chronik*, rose from 90.96 in 1908 to 94.85 marks in 1909, and those of stocks from 145.34 to 156.96 marks. The Paris bourse paralleled this activity in 1909 as a result of the ease that prevailed in money rates, the relative absence of American commitments, and the clearing up of domestic political problems. The 3 per cent Rentes which had increased during 1908 from 94.3 to 97.6, stood at 96.7 in the beginning of 1909 and reached 98.67 francs by the close of the year. The 4½ per cent Russian bonds, floated in January at 89¼ francs, stepped over par in November, in spite of the fact that $262 millions of these bonds were floated in 1909. The bourse also showed marked interest in the stocks of industrial, railroad, and electrical companies. The average price of 163 securities, computed by the *Economiste Européen,* indicates a rise of 2.55 per cent over the average price of the same securities the previous year. The London stock exchange remained somewhat slack in comparison with those of Continental countries. It received an impetus, however, during the second half of the year, from the remarkable advance in May of Kaffir gold mining shares,—this advance being due to economies adopted in operating the mines. Four minor "booms"—one in American Rails, one in Kaffirs, one in West Africans, and another in Rubber shares,—added further buoyancy to the London market. This belated activity was the result of sporadic business revivals in first one industry and then another.[1] The market felt considerable congestion of new and old securities, and sought to unburden itself by selling abroad, and by stimulating domestic absorption through larger imports of gold. Nevertheless, prices of stocks showed a fair amount of firmness, and considerable advances occurred in the last half of the year. The rise in the average price of 387 securities, as computed by the *London Bankers Magazine,* was 2 per cent for 1909.

Developments in the Credit Market. The ease in the money market which, as we have seen, developed in 1908, prevailed in the United States until August, 1909. Both time and call money rates descended during the first half of the year to a level lower than those that had obtained in the previous year. This is evidenced from a perusal of the following table:

[1] *Cf. London Economist,* vol. lxx, pp. 9-11.

AVERAGE MONTHLY INTEREST RATES ON THE MONEY MARKETS OF NEW YORK, BERLIN, PARIS AND LONDON IN 1909

	New York		Berlin		Paris		London	
	Call rate	*60-90 day paper*	*Bank*	*Market*	*Bank*	*Market*	*Bank*	*Market*
January	1.81%	3.68%	4.00%	2.24%	3.00%	2.47%	2.87%	2.57%
March	1.85	3.50	3.50	2.66	3.00	1.23	2.90	2.01
July	2.06	3.38	3.50	2.28	3.00	1.26	2.50	1.39
August	2.17	4.04	3.50	2.13	3.00	1.25	2.50	1.45
November ..	4.65	5.09	5.00	4.47	3.00	2.82	5.00	4.23
December ..	5.03	5.09	5.00	4.34	3.00	2.75	4.60	3.72

In the latter part of August, sudden advances occurred and a sharp stringency ensued, lasting from September until December. There were several reasons for this sudden tension in the credit market. A demand for funds arose from the interior for purposes of crop movement. Gold exports (mainly to Paris and Argentina until May and to South America continuously throughout the year, largely upon European account), assumed great proportions, totaling $132,881,000 for the year, in contrast to imports amounting to $44,087,000; selling of American securities on foreign account further drained the gold supply; and considerable liquidation on the stock exchange took place in August. A great and persistent demand for funds grew out of the world-wide revival in production and trade, and the moderate degrees of speculation in securities and commodities, especially in Germany, that followed. This brought an unexpected raising of discount rates by the Reichsbank and the Bank of England in October, these being inaugurated in part to protect gold reserves from the demands of South America and Egypt, and to restrain American borrowing in Europe for stock exchange and commodity speculation. It is evident that the great growth of foreign trade, during 1909, the tremendous increase in this country of imports in proportion to exports, and the creation of favorable credit balances here through the selling of American securities, caused a heavy outflow of gold, either to Europe directly or to South America on European account. The extent of the gold outflow is here presented:

UNITED STATES' BALANCE OF TRADE IN 1909 AND GOLD MOVEMENTS

(IN MILLION DOLLARS)

	Exports	*Imports*	*Excess of exports*	*Gold balance*
1907	$1,923	$1,423	$500	+ $88
1908	1,753	1,116	637	− 31
1909	1,701	1,476	225	− 89

Foreign exchange rates advanced in New York, during the last three months of the year, because of the continued selling of securities on foreign account, and because of the large number of finance bills drawn during the summer months against the probable cotton and grain remittances to be expected in the fall which had been overestimated.

While the increasing volume of production and trade, activity upon the stock market, heavy issues of new securities, and higher prices prevailing for commodities and securities, were primarily instrumental in producing a growing quantity of funds, the heavy outflow of gold, on the other hand, stood in the way of any great increase in bank reserves. (Gold was the only noticeable variable in our monetary system.) In proportion to the country's growth in volume of business, following the recovery from the panic of 1907, our supply of monetary stock remained almost negligible—approximately $50,000,000, up to May, 1910. The banking organization remained unchanged, however, except for a greater efficiency in the use of bank credit. But this was not sufficient to offset the failure of reserves to meet the growing demands for credit. The reserve ratio of cash holdings to individual deposits of all national banks,

INDEX NUMBERS OF PRODUCTION, WHOLESALE PRICES, MONEY STOCK IN THE UNITED STATES, AND THE WORLD'S GOLD PRODUCTION [1]

1911–1913 = 100

	Production	Price	Money Stock	World's gold production (1890-99 = 100)
1905	86	87	76	196
1906	91	90	81	205
1907	89	95	86	210
1908	84	92	93	225
1909	94	98	94	231
1910	96	101	94	231
1911	93	96	98	235
1912	106	102	100	237
1913	101	101	102	234
1914	101	101	103	223

—not including checks and exchanges—fell from 20.0 per cent on May 14, 1908, to 15.1 per cent on November 16, 1909. The percentage of clearing house bank reserves in New York fell from its high point of 29.62 per cent in August, 1908, to 25.54 per cent in November, 1909.

The European money situation presented a similar aspect, —a relative ease prevailed until the fall of the year.[2] In Paris, the money market did not even then experience a stringency. The abnormally large imports of gold to France in 1908, (which continued to a certain extent during the first few months of 1909,) as a result of the large accumulations of interest on foreign investments,—accumulations which could be offset neither by balance of

[1] Money stock index computed from *Comptroller's Reports*. Production index is that of Walter W. Stewart. Prices from Bureau of Labor Statistics. World's gold production as given by the Director of the Mint. *Cf.* W. W. Stewart, "Index Number of Production," *Am. Econ. Rev. Sup.*, March, 1921.

[2] *Cf. London Economist*, vol. lxix, pp. 739 and 903; *cf. Volkswirtschaftliche Chronik*, 1909, p. 926.

trade nor by foreign reinvestment—were quite sufficient to keep money rates low. The figures below, showing the excess in imports of commodities and gold, as well as the specie holding of the Bank of France, indicate the favorable condition of the French money market:

	Mdse.	*Gold*	*Reserves of Bank of France*
	(IN MILLION DOLLARS)		
1907	$121	$56	$709
1908	114	192	764
1909	101	35	873
1910	181	11	823

The Paris market was furthermore able to take care of the huge Russian loans, and to make—reluctantly it must be admitted—some advances to the Bank of England in November. Loans to Americans had been refused on account of the heavy speculation in securities and commodities going on here. Yet the Bank of France, in spite of its huge gold accumulations, refused in the fall to lend freely to meet the requirements of trade and industry. Political considerations were in all likelihood responsible for this policy.

The English money market manifested varied characteristics during 1909, as the result of the world-wide recovery from business depression. The revival of industry and trade, the need of funds for moving crops, higher prices, and large capital investments,—all produced a stringency in the fall. Heavy demands for gold were making themselves felt in London, and higher rates, to protect the reserves of the Bank of England, became necessary. Even so, it was possible to give some aid to New York bankers in the fall. In Germany, where business improvement had proceeded further and speculation had gotten under way, a similar scarcity of funds arose. This sharp demand for capital went hand in hand with the Reichsbank's policy of increasing and maintaining its gold holdings to produce higher interest rates. Increases in governmental budgets, for purposes of naval, military, and social programs, gave rise to influences that affected the monetary situation all over Europe, which, together with demands for private and foreign capital, converged to produce the moderate financial strain which occupied the latter part of 1909.

Growth of Production and Trade. We have seen how production and trade gave sporadic manifestations of improvement in the United States during the closing months of 1908.[1] It is to be noted, however, that there occurred a marked hesitancy in industrial and commercial activities in the opening months of 1909. This hesitancy was due in part to the prospect of tariff revisions, and the cutting of prices in the steel industry, over a period of three months. Overproduction in the copper trade also played its roll, and labor difficulties in the anthracite coal regions added their weight of influence temporarily against business expansion. By the end of the first three months, however, caution was abandoned and production and trade continued to gather volume until the close of the year.

The volume of bank clearings outside of New York, were the manifestation of a decided growth of business transactions throughout the year, and indicated a particularly great expansion in the fall. Gross earnings of railroads in that period corroborate this growth of industry and trade. Foreign commerce statistics show a marked expansion in imports, and a comparative diminishing of exports. These indexes are given below:

[1] *Cf. supra*, p. 35.

Relative Imports, Bank Clearings Outside of New York and Gross Earnings of Railroads in the United States

1890-99 = 100

	Imports	Gross earnings of railroads [1]	Clearings outside of New York
1907	187	223	236
1908	147	206	217
1909	194	208	254

(Adapted from Mitchell's *Business Cycles.* Also see Stewart's *Index Number of Production* given on page 43.)

The items of increase in imports were largely raw materials, and, to a smaller extent, foodstuffs. This was the result of the earlier revival of industries here, and the higher prices paid here as compared with those prevailing in Europe, which caused raw materials to seek a market in this country. The first six months of 1909 were dull for the coal trade. The prospect of labor difficulties to develop in April, 1909, brought about production of anthracite coal in 1908 for storage against that time; and overproduction resulted when labor troubles failed to become acute, as expected by the operators. The last half of the year 1909 saw the coal industry in a state of great activity, cold weather and the revival of industry stimulating the demand. The production of anthracite coal increased 6½ per cent while that of bituminous decreased 3½ per cent over that of 1908, both falling short of the 1907 totals.

Reports of copper smelters during this period indicate that copper production in 1909 advanced over the previous year. Copper consumption was resumed in America, and the revival of the electrical industries in Germany

[1] Gross earnings are given for year ending, June 30. The absolute figures in million dollars for year ending, December 30 are as follows:

1907	$2,343
1908	2,303
1909	2,582

brought good orders from abroad, so that brass, sheet, wire, and tube mills worked overtime to fill orders.

Iron and steel production was stimulated by the price readjustment which took place during April and May, 1909, following the breaking of the price maintenance policy of the leading interests, during the first three or four months of the year. Unfilled orders of the United States Steel Corporation mounted immediately after this price reduction. Production of pig iron reacted in a similar fashion, and increased rapidly as the year passed.[1]

PRODUCTION OF METALS IN UNITED STATES—1909

	Copper	*Pig iron*	*Unfinished orders of U. S. Steel Corporation*
	millions of lbs.	*thousands of gross tons*	*thousands of tons*
January	112	1,117	——
March	117	1,140	3,543
June	117	1,365	4,058
September ..	121	1,660	4,798
December ..	118	1,768	5,927

The yield of crops in 1909 was not out of the ordinary, except for oats, which jumped all records. Corn and cotton yields were lower than they had been for four or five years. Wheat brought a good yield. There had been a noticeable decrease of acreage in corn, wheat, and cotton. Extraordinarily high prices prevailed in this country for grain during the year. In the foreign crop-producing countries, statistics indicate a fair yield of corn, especially in Austria-Hungary and Argentina. Wheat yields were very good in Russia, India, Canada, and France, though somewhat small for Austria, Argentina, and Germany. Whatever shortage there was, in the cotton yield of the United States, was made good by the extraordinary yield in India.[2]

[1] For statistics on general production *cf. supra*, p. 43.

[2] *Bureau of Crop Estimates*, U. S. Department of Agriculture.

Industry in the European countries did not recover from the depression developed during 1908 until the second half of 1909; the upswing in production and trade, as indicated by the bank clearings of Paris, London, and the German Reichsbank, were delayed until fall. The figures for clearings as well as for unemployment are summarized in the following tables:

PARIS AND LONDON BANKS' CLEARINGS AND THE CLEARINGS OF THE REICHSBANK

(IN MILLION DOLLARS)

	Paris		*London*		*Reichsbank*	
	1908	*1909*	*1908*	*1909*	*1908*	*1909*
January	$442	$476	$5,454	$5,556	$944	$1,056
May	374	445	4,754	5,049	886	1,037
August	384	406	4,414	4,943	820	896
November	423	520	4,823	5,667	856	980

Unemployment statistics also lead to the conclusion that the industrial and trade recovery in Europe was not of any far-reaching importance until the second half of 1909:

UNEMPLOYMENT IN GERMANY, FRANCE AND ENGLAND

	Germany			*France*			*England*		
	1907	*1908*	*1909*	*1907*	*1908*	*1909*	*1907*	*1908*	*1909*
January	1.7	2.9	4.2	7.8	10.9	13.5	3.9	5.8	8.7
May	1.4	2.8	2.8	5.9	11.9	6.8	3.0	7.4	7.9
August	1.4	2.7	2.3	7.5	8.2	6.4	3.6	8.5	7.7
November	1.7	3.2	2.0	9.4	9.4	6.6	4.5	8.7	6.5

Germany—percentage of collective trade-union members—*Reichs Arbeitsblatt.*

France—percentage of unemployed, per hundred, of trade-union members—*Bulletin Le Ministere Du Travail.*

England—percentage of trade-union members unemployed at end of month—*Board of Trade Labor Gazette.*

Statistics of production in the particular industries show a greater increase in volume in Germany than they do in France and England. Coal and pig iron production in

Germany increased from 212 millions of long tons of coal in 1908, to 214 in 1909; pig iron increased from 11,600,000 long tons to 12,400,000. In France, coal production remained at 37,000,000 long tons; that of pig iron increased from 3,400,000 to 3,500,000 long tons. In the United Kingdom, coal production increased from 262,000,000 to 264,000,000 long tons, pig iron from 9,100,000 to 9,500,000. Bills of exchange in circulation in Germany increased from $7,030 millions to $7,940 millions, and in France from $7,510 millions to $7,780 millions. Germany's unfavorable balance of trade was greater than in 1908, for imports, especially in raw materials, increased. Imports and exports, in France, increased markedly, resulting in a smaller unfavorable balance than had occurred for two years. For the United Kingdom, the unfavorable balance of trade bulked large. Exports of manufactured articles remained static, while the imports of foods, and especially of raw materials, increased. However, the export trade recovered considerably during the latter part of the year.[1]

The Rise in Commodity Prices. Prices of general commodities at wholesale and at retail presented continuous rise during the year 1909, following their recovery in September of the previous year. During the last four months, especially, this upward movement was particularly noticeable. The increase in prices, according to the Bureau of Labor Statistics Index Numbers from August, 1908, to December, 1909, for commodities at wholesale, was from 121.4 to 132.2, while from August to December, 1909, the rise was from 126.4 to 132.2, and for commodities at retail, from 83.4 to 91.1.[2] An analysis of the separate groups

[1] *Cf. supra*, p. 30 for other indexes on business expansion in Europe. That the business revival was in its incipient stages in Europe during 1909 is evidenced by the heavy imports of raw materials.

[2] It must be noted that the number and kind of commodities at wholesale and at retail in these index numbers are not the same.

of commodities reveals the fact that prices of farm products increased phenomenally from 132.7 in September, 1908, to 169.2 in December, 1909; those of raw materials for the same period from 125.6 to 143.1, and prices of manufactured products from 120.9 to 129.5. It is interesting to note the difference between the price developments of these three groups of commodities, and especially significant is a comparison of the farm products price trend, with that of the remaining two groups. The rise in the prices of farm products, may be explained by the poor yield of cotton, the moderate grain crops, and the increasing prices of food products all over the world. The abortive increase in prices of pig iron, in the fall of 1908, met with a reaction between January and April of 1909, but later responded with marked vigor, after steel prices had been readjusted upon a lower level. By restriction of output, prices of copper remained steady at about 13 cents a pound, —the profitable producing point at this time. The market was in a sensitive condition because of the constant influence of the speculative interest in London.[1]

The marked rise in price of farm products and of raw materials greatly increased the costs of materials of industries. In addition, the increases in wage scales, and rising interest rates, encroached further upon the margins of profit. This led to an increase in the demand for credit from the industries at large. The resulting financial strain upon our seemingly inadequate banking resources, will be considered in a subsequent chapter.

In Europe, the price movement took on a different aspect, in that the recovery was much slower there than in this country. During the first half of 1909, industry and trade remained relatively inactive, the physical volume of business showing little evidence of increase, and the general trend of

[1] *Cf. Mineral Industry*, vol. xviii, p. 149.

commodity prices being downward. Available price index numbers for 1909 show a rise in prices for England and France, and little change, or only a slight decline, for those in Germany.[1] In the former countries the rise took place in the second half year.[2] In Germany, the prices of 23 items of consumers' commodities increased from 112 in 1908, to 114 in 1909; those of 21 items of producers' goods decreased from 123 to 121, while three index numbers of general prices show a decrease for the year, under those of 1908. It is a notable fact that the price recovery in England and France was relatively slight, in comparison with that in the United States, while, on the other hand, prices in Germany declined during the greater part of the year, and did not recover until the closing months of 1909, when they manifested a sharp rise. This condition led to the great volume of imports previously referred to.

Demand for Commercial and Investment Funds. The volume of loans and discounts by national banks in the United States increased markedly during the year, as a result of the business expansion, although, in the fall months, the rate of increase slackened because of the depletion of reserves, and the resulting tension in the investment market. The contraction of loans in September and thereafter seems to have been confined principally to the clearing house banks of New York. Their reserves fell, as above indicated, which resulted in higher interest rates and a curtailment of loans, which in turn led to a decline in the prices of securities.[3] The extent of the above changes in the condition of bank credit may be seen in the following figures:

[1] England—Sauerbeck; France—Domergue; Germany—computed from data in the *Vierteljahrshefte zur Statistik des Deutschen Reichs.*

[2] The London Economist's Index Number of Wholesale Prices indicates that the beginning price rise occurred in May. *Cf. supra*, p. 25.

[3] *Cf. supra*, p. 43.

LOANS AND DISCOUNTS AND ACTUAL RESERVE RATIO OF ALL NATIONAL BANKS AND NEW YORK CLEARING HOUSE BANKS

ALL NATIONAL BANKS				NEW YORK CLEARING HOUSE BANKS	
	Loans and discounts million dollars on reporting dates	*Reserve ratio*		*Loans and discounts million dollars* average for month	*Reserve ratio*
Feb. 5	$4,870	18.3%	: Feb.	$1,325	25.90%
Apr. 28	4,988	18.2	: Apr.	1,339	25.80
June 23	5,061	18.1	: June	1,351	26.77
Sept. 1	5,158	17.0	: Sept.	1,330	25.66
Nov. 16 ...	5,191	15.1	: Nov.	1,218	25.54

Analysis of the reports of European banks brings to light no such great expansion in loans. In fact, the Joint Stock Banks of England and Wales show a decrease in acceptance liabilities and in discounts and advances, during the period of May to November, 1909, from 205 to 180 million dollars and from 2,081 to 2,069 million dollars, respectively. Deposits and current accounts, however, increased from 3,283 million dollars to 3,303. The loan-and-discount item of the Bank of France indicates a similar trend, while cash reserves and circulation expanded considerably. A similar relation between loan-and-discount items and cash reserves is characteristic of the Reichsbank reports, while the yield of the stamp tax on bills of exchange, according to these same reports, shows a marked increase for the year (part of this increase being attributable to the change in the method of calculating the tax).[1] A closer persual of European bank statistics gives evidence of a greater expansion in bank loans in Germany

[1] Increase over the preceding year in significant items of the combined statements of the German Joint Stock Banks in million dollars:

	1908	*1909*
Advances and contangoes	+ $63	+ $141
Acceptances and cheques	— 20	+ 9
Deposits on current accounts	+ 4	+ 97

than in the two other countries, and a greater increase in French banks than in those of England. During the latter part of the year, however, marked increases in the use of bank credit were noticeable in all European countries.

Volume of Security Issues. The ample supply of loanable funds during the first nine months of the year was met with a heavy issue of securities. The total of new issues in Germany and England remained somewhat below the high totals of 1908, but was exceedingly large, while in the United States and France, the new issues far exceeded those of the previous year. Although issues of new stocks increased remarkably, government issues receded in all capital markets:

SECURITY ISSUES IN GERMANY, FRANCE AND ENGLAND[1]

(IN MILLION DOLLARS)

				Private	
FRANCE	*Total*	*Foreign Gov'ts*	*Home Gov'ts*	*Stocks*	*Bonds*
1907	$569	$204	$12	$193	$160
1908	698	223	19	212	244
1909	842	189	30	391	232
GERMANY				*(Dividenden Papiere*	*(Festverzinsliche-Werte*
1907	$480	$19	$234	$100	$127
1908	795	44	430	85	236
1909	770	41	347	122	259
ENGLAND				*Private*	
1907	$593	$102	$32	$459	
1908	935	119	51	765	
1909	887	107	42	738	

The numerous applications for long time loans in Europe, as well as in this country, brought about accentuated de-

[1] Statistics for Germany were compiled from the *Deutsche Oekonomist*; for England, from the *London Economist*; and for France from *L'Economiste Européen*. For new issues in United States, *cf. supra*, p. 31.

mands for investment funds.[1] As has been noted, bank loans in Europe, especially in England and France, did not reach the extent of expansion attained in the United States, for the reason that our industrial and trade revival was so much more marked, and our rise in prices so much greater. As may be seen, the credit market in the United States suffered a twofold demand for funds,—for investment and for commercial purposes.

The influences operating in the European and American capital markets are described thus by M. Arthur Raffalovitch:[2]

There is no formula for the year of 1909 — Factors operating diverse and contradictory — Public finance of Europe is in a bad state and great demands of capital by governments occurred—Political disturbances in Balkans, Persia, Spain, etc., caused military and naval expenditures — Demands of public finance squelched private initiative and capital supply was compromised between public and private needs — There were complaints against the growing burden of taxation — Capital emigrated at an increased rate and sought foreign stock investments—Markets of securities and commodities nevertheless showed revival — New security issues absorbed most of floating capital—The tenacity of American optimism was striking—Then excessive use of credit and issues of new securities resulted—This brought a premature reaction as an economic corrective in view of the over-investment.

Construction Activity and Commercial Failures of the United States. Building permits issued in 206 cities of the United States, show a remarkable expansion in construction activity. Monthly values of building permits, issued for twenty cities, also indicate a large amount of con-

[1] *Cf. supra*, p. 32.

[2] *Commercial and Financial Chronicle*, vol. xci, p. 555.

struction; but these figures show a gradual shading off during the second half of 1909.[1] This shading off may be taken as evidence that the tension upon the investment market at the close of the year exerted a depressing influence upon those industries engaged in the making of producers' goods. The number of commercial failures in the United States, according to Bradstreet's reports, decreased considerably, and a similar decrease in commercial failures was noticeable in Europe.

[1] *Harvard Review of Economic Statistics*; *cf. supra*, p. 31.

CHAPTER III

The Recurring Depression of 1910-1911

A halting and sporadic revival of business is often characteristic of the transition from a state of depression to one of business prosperity. The United States antedated foreign countries by five or six months, in passing through this preliminary stage, and business in this country gathered volume and buoyancy far in excess and in advance of Europe, during 1909. But this prosperity in the United States was not destined to be long continued. While industry, in European countries, in spite of a later revival, reached the full tide of prosperity, (except perhaps in France, where poor harvests left an unfavorable impress upon business conditions), the United States relapsed into a period of depression at the very beginning of 1910.[1] Recession continued until the closing months of 1911, when manifestations of recovery again became noticeable. Unavoidably, such a reaction made itself felt in European business conditions. However, the spheres of production and trade were but slightly affected in those countries, while the consequences of our relapse spent their full force in European investment markets.

The Liquidation in the Security Markets. The first signs of the business reaction occurred, as usual, on the stock exchange. The increase in prices of industrial and of medium

[1] *Volkswirtschaftliche Chronik*, 1910, p. 885; *Commercial and Financial Chronicle*, vol. xli, p. 5; *London Economist*, vol. lxx. p. 73; *L'Economiste Francais*, vol. xxxviii, pp. 758 and 797.

grade transportation stocks culminated, as we have seen, during September, October and November of 1909, thus ending their meteoric rise dating from December, 1907; while those of the better grade transportation stocks maintained their advance until the close of the year. The characteristic course of general stock prices is illustrated in the following data:

AVERAGE PRICES OF 12 INDUSTRIAL AND 20 RAILROAD STOCKS
Wall Street Journal

	Industrial stocks				*Railroad stocks*			
	1908	*1909*	*1910*	*1911*	*1908*	*1909*	*1910*	*1911*
Jan.	62.7	85.6	94.5	83.3	92.8	118.9	125.4	116.8
May	72.5	90.3	87.2	84.5	101.2	124.8	120.2	119.6
Aug.	83.0	97.8	78.8	82.2	107.6	131.6	112.0	117.2
Oct.	81.6	98.1	83.0	76.8	108.0	130.0	116.4	112.8
Dec.	85.6	98.0	81.0	80.9	117.6	128.2	112.9	116.6

The prices of industrial and railroad stocks reached their lowest point in July and August, 1910, respectively, and, after a moderate increase in price, sank together to a very low level, in September, 1911.[1] Nevertheless, during this intermediate period, prices of stocks exhibited firmness, maintaining themselves at a level approximately 50 per cent above the lowest average range reached in the later months of 1907 and earlier months of 1908. Prices and sales of

[1] Relative prices of 40 railroad stocks and 10 railroad bonds as computed by Mitchell:

	Stocks				*Bonds*	
	1910		*1911*		*1910*	*1911*
	low	*high*	*low*	*high*		
Jan.	262	298	246	262	111.1	109.1
May	252	272	249	263	108.4	108.9
Aug.	*228*	250	232	262	*107.6*	108.7
Oct.	247	266	*232*	*246*	109.5	*107.5*
Dec.	243	255	240	252	108.7	110.1

Compare with tables on pages 16 and 37.

stocks declined continuously during 1910, and until August, 1911. Subsequently, having struck bottom almost simultaneously in the late summer of 1911, they increased again very moderately for the remainder of that year, because of the better profits of industries and the relative cheapness of credit. Bond prices moved sympathetically with stock prices during this period, although their volume of sales on the stock exchange showed only a moderate increase from September, 1910, throughout 1911, following the decline since the beginning of 1909 in both prices and sales. The course of bond prices synchronized with that of interest rates.

Call money rates eased off sharply in February, 1910, and remained at a low level throughout the depression, thus relieving the stock market of the tension that developed during the latter months of 1909, when prices of securities were highest and liquidation was beginning to set in. Time money rates, on the other hand, remained high and even became quite tense in the fall of 1910. Equally unfavorable was the condition of the clearing house banks' reserves. These reserves diminished considerably during the latter part of 1909 and continued low during 1910. Selling of foreign-held securities in our market had proceeded in great volume before the dip in security prices during the closing months of the previous year; but this selling was quite absent during 1910-11, except for a short season of selling on foreign account, instigated by the rise in discount rates abroad, in August, 1911. It is alleged by some that the active trust prosecutions and anti-trust legislation that took place at that time, and the impairment of business confidence by Taft's strict adherence to Roosevelt's policies, were the causes of the decline of the security market.[1] It is true that these factors did operate during the year 1909, but they

[1] *Financial Review—Commercial and Finance Chronicle*, vol. xci, p. 10.

had practically no effect upon the activity in the security market.

The European bourses reflected to some degree the depressed condition of the New York stock market. Especially were those securities affected in which over-speculation had occurred. The Berlin bourse was laboring under an overissue of securities floated during previous years, particularly at the beginning of 1910. The quietness of the security market during the early part of the year was broken in May, owing to a spurt in the prices of electrical and railroad stocks. Conditions were ripe for an upswing in security prices since the process of price levelling had been accomplished as a result of the large emissions in Berlin, and the decline of the security market in New York. A recurrent laxity appeared during the fourth quarter, as a result of tight money. The taxes on sales on the bourses (*Börsenumsatzsteuern*) indicate an increasing volume of security sales throughout 1910 and 1911. In the latter year, the bourse stood between two opposing influences—industrial healthfulness, on the one hand, and political disturbances, on the other. During the last half of the year pessimistic influences were the stronger. Active speculation in Berlin, Vienna, and St. Petersburg, during the first part of 1911, resulting in large gains in stock prices, was neutralized to a great extent by the disturbing political situation, and the resulting credit contraction in the fall. The tension in the money market further operated to halt the buoyancy of the stock exchange, and the sudden liquidation instigated by political apprehensions very nearly caused a panic in October. The course of the average prices of all the interest-bearing and dividend-yielding securities on the Berlin bourse is given below:

1909	*Interest-bearing*	*Dividend-yielding*
Yearly average	94.85 marks	156.96 marks
1910		
1st quarter	95.10	163.04
2nd quarter	94.73	162.19
3rd quarter	94.62	162.58
4th quarter	94.59	163.28
Yearly average	94.76	162.77
1911		
1st quarter	95.04	164.91
2nd quarter	94.88	163.28
3rd quarter	94.00	160.35
4th quarter	93.43	161.27
Yearly average	94.34	162.45

The Paris bourse also stood between two opposing influences: cheap credit, on the one hand, and the heavy issues of securities in 1910, coupled with poor agricultural conditions, on the other. The resultant was a general decline in security values. The *Economiste Européen* reported a fall in the average price of 163 securities of 1.55 per cent in 1910, against a rise of 2.55 per cent in 1909. Railroad securities and *Rentes* lost, chiefly, while bank and industrial securities made some advances. *Rentes,* 3 per cent, were quoted at 99.22 francs in December, 1909, and sank to 96.47 in October, 1910. The investor shifted his interest from foreign securities to domestic issues. The crop failure and great railroad strike militated against favorable developments upon the bourse, and all speculative influences were ineffectual during the second half year. During the first half of 1911, the bourse underwent some favorable developments. Speculation increased, especially in Russian securities, which began to improve at St. Petersburg. Dividend-stock reacted strongly, reflecting the industrial activity, while interest-bearing securities developed weakness. In the second part of the year, prices declined, and the bourse approached something very like a panic. The effects of the overspeculation that had occurred in Berlin, Vienna, and St. Petersburg were being felt. The sharp decline in the American security market also reacted upon the bourses at Berlin and Paris, where a large volume of American securities was held. These factors, in addition to the increasing price of credit, exerted a somewhat unfavorable influence upon the security market in France. The average price of the 163 securities, mentioned above, underwent a further downward revision of 2.07 per cent in 1911.

Things were not as well with the London security market as they were elsewhere in Europe in the years 1910-11. During the first part of 1910, the volume of sales was large, and the rise in security prices kept pace until April. Oil and rubber shares, especially, in which excessive speculation occurred, showed great gains. But during the remainder of the year there was a rather general lowering of security prices. The zenith, then, in London security prices, was reached several months before the rise culminated in the Continental market. In the decline which began after April, American railroad securities were principally involved with foreign bonds, South American and copper shares. British railroad and industrial stocks continued to hold good prices. The 2½ per cent consols stood at 82.93 in January and at 78.58 in December. The higher interest rates that prevailed on foreign capital issues and the greater prosperity that ruled in other countries had a depressing effect upon the older, fixed, interest-bearing securities. In 1911 the London stock exchange reacted sympathetically with other security markets. The collapse of the boom in oil and rubber shares during August, 1910, had dampened speculation considerably. Liquidation and the revision of prices upon the New York stock market exerted a depressing influence. Still, great advances occurred in the prices of British and Canadian railroad securities in 1911, while those of copper shares gained slightly, and industrials held their own. Later in the year, 1911, the financial strain caused by a mild panic upon the Berlin bourse, due to the Moroccan trouble and the sudden recall of French loans, estimated to have been between 70 and 100 million dollars, produced a depression in the market. This loss of funds was largely offset by American bankers, who loaned a considerable quantity of funds to the German banks during the latter part of the year. These disturbances, resulting largely from war scares that caused a heavy liquidation of securities upon the continent, exerted their depressing influence also upon the London exchange toward the close of 1911. The decline in the average price of 387 securities in 1910 and 1911 was 2.07 per cent and 0.60 per cent, respectively. The prices had, however, regained 2.01 per cent from December, 1910, to April, 1911, but by the end of the year had again decreased 2.61 per cent.

Influences Operating in the Credit Market. The money market in the United States, during 1910, was characterized by rather high rates on time-money and low rates on call-money. The year began with a relaxation in the price of credit; but almost immediately, a sharp advance in rates on time-money set in. In call-money, on the other hand, rates declined continuously until fall. The trend of interest rates is given below:

AVERAGE TIME AND CALL LOAN RATES AT NEW YORK

	1910			*1911*		
	Call	*60–90 days*	*4–6 mos.*	*Call*	*60–90 days*	*4–6 mos.*
Feb.	2.78%	4.44%	5.16%	3.18%	4.09%	4.72%
Aug.	1.55	5.43	6.30	2.31	4.19	4.86
Nov.	3.23	5.50	6.15	2.72	3.91	4.72
Dec.	3.38	4.66	5.28	4.03	4.63	5.25

The declining prices and sales of securities on the stock exchange, as well as the unwillingness on the part of the New York banks to loan money on time, in the face of an almost static volume of reserves, were responsible for these low rates in call-loan money. The reserves of the New York clearing house banks, which had greatly diminished during the latter part of 1909, remained low during 1910. Loans and deposits followed a similar course.

RESERVES AND DEPOSITS OF NEW YORK CLEARING HOUSE BANKS
(IN MILLION DOLLARS)

	1909			*1910*			*1911*		
	Deposits	*Reserves*	*Reserve ratio*	*Deposits*	*Reserves*	*Reserve ratio*	*Deposits*	*Reserves*	*Reserve ratio*
. ....	$1,385	$372	26.96%	$1,206	$324	26.89%	$1,245	$339	27.26%
y	1,426	390	27.39	1,189	329	27.70	1,429	368	25.77
ıt. ...	1,360	349	25.66	1,280	341	26.63	1,384	369	26.64
:.	1,170	302	25.79	1,192	305	25.62	1,298	336	25.84
				Of All National Banks					
ı.	——	——	——	5,194	836	15.9%	5,119	839	16.3%
).	4,701	863	18.3%	——	——	——	——	——	——
r. ...	——	——	——	5,229	838	15.9	5,306	911	17.1
r. ...	4,824	881	18.2	——	——	——	——	——	——
ıe	4,900	889	18.1	5,302	824	15.5	5,480	949	17.3
ıt. ...	5,012	857	17.0	5,147	855	16.6	5,492	899	16.4
v. ...	5,122	808	15.1	5,306	819	15.4	——	——	——
:. ...	——	——	——	——	——	——	5,537	866	15.6

The interior banks drew heavily upon their funds in the banks of reserve cities and continued to expand their loans, while their deposits diminished to some extent. Their reserves remained low during the whole of 1910. Gold exports, which had begun to decrease toward the close of 1909, balanced imports for 1910. In April, 1910, an exportation of $36,284,000 took place, brought about because the Bank of England advanced the price of American eagles in order to attract the metal to meet the heavy commercial and investment demands for funds. The gold movements for that year are to be attributed chiefly to the heavy demand for gold in the London gold market, by countries outside of Europe, a demand which eventually made itself felt in other markets. In addition to this, there were the bounteous early harvests in India, Russia the United States, and especially Argentina; there were heavy security issues in the fall of 1910; and the heavy demand for gold and funds in the United States, due to the industrial revival abroad. All these factors broke upon the credit market stimultaneously during the fall of 1910.

Time-money rates in the United States began to ease off sharply in December, 1910, and during 1911 both call- and time-loan rates reached almost the low level of 1908. This lowering in rates of interest was due to the increase in our gold supply and the moderate inactivity of industry in this country. Gold imports remained in excess of exports from May, 1910, to October, 1911. Exports of commodities made large gains after the middle of 1910, and continued to gain throughout 1911, while the volume of imports showed little change. This favorable balance of trade operated to increase our gold supply, (an increase that was reflected in the reserve holdings of banks, which were augmented during the first half of 1911), and in the growing monetary stock in the United States.[1] Funds found only a limited market throughout the greater part of 1911, and loaning of funds abroad, where the increase in business activity continued uninterruptedly, became widely practiced.

Conditions in European Credit Markets. Interest rates in the money markets of Europe seemed to bear a very loose relation to those of this country. The market rates in Germany, France, and England were, in general, somewhat higher in 1910 than in 1911, and showed the normal seasonal rise, paralled also by bank rates during the fall

[1] *Cf. supra*, p. 43.

months of each year. Their course is presented in the following table of averages for four months:

	Berlin				*Paris*				*London*		
	1910		*1911*		*1910*		*1911*		*1910*		*191.*
	Bank	*Market*	*Bank*	*Market*	*Bank*	*Market*	*Bank*	*Market*	*Bank*	*Market*	*Bank M*
.. ..	4.75	3.09	5.00	3.50	3.00	2.63	3.00	2.62	3.75	3.93	4.30
y	4.00	3.19	4.00	2.84	3.00	2.17	3.00	2.13	4.00	3.51	3.00
t.	4.50	3.85	4.50	4.16	3.00	2.38	3.25	3.08	3.25	3.06	3.50
v.	5.00	4.50	5.00	4.51	3.00	2.80	3.50	3.33	4.90	4.31	4.00

Rates oscillated within narrower limits abroad than they did here. In Germany, increasing unfavorable trade balances caused gold imports to decrease. The decline in 1908-09-10 and 1911, respectively, was from $77 to $70 to $45 to $31 millions. Reserves, however, increased and the German money market became more independent,—which had been its aim,—of other countries. Although the market-rate in the first half of 1911 indicated a greater ease of money than 1910 had seen, the bank-rate was maintained on the level of the former year. In the fall of 1911, however, a sharp advance occurred, caused by the need for money to repay large foreign loans, and by the increasing sales which took place in the security market, together with the rise of commodity prices and the growth of industrial activity.[1] Much of the stringency was relieved, however, by the loans from American bankers, and by the fact that the Reichsbank employed foreign bills in the payment of foreign claims. Interest rates were thereby kept within normal limits.

There was no sound basis for an upswing in business in France during 1910, because of poor crops and the railroad strike. Nevertheless, some improvements were made.

[1] The *Vossische Zeitung* estimates that the funds withdrawn from Germany by France alone during the last half of 1911 amounted to $200 millions.

The huge gold imports of previous years had allowed money to remain fairly easy during the first part of the year, though rates were much higher than they had been in 1909. In the fall, the market rate approached the official rate, for the reason that considerable French capital had been attracted by the higher rates abroad; and because an increasingly unfavorable balance of trade had resulted from the crop failure. Significance is to be attached to the changed status of the Bank of France in relation to the rise in the market-rate of discount. On the one hand, the Bank lost strikingly in specie and foreign money, and on the other hand showed a marked increase in loans and securities and bills of exchange. As the year progressed, there developed a strong competition between the low interest-bearing domestic securities and the foreign issues, with the result that French capital emigrated, as the high exchange rates and the outflow of gold indicate. In addition, the great commercial banks, in their business of underwriting the heavy foreign security issues, required considerable reserves to meet the short-time credit demands so incurred. These factors all operated to produce a strained credit condition toward the close of 1910. Although money rates remained low during the fore part of 1911, the Paris market felt an increasing strain during the fall months. Heavy imports continued until July, because of the poor crops in 1910, which still operated somewhat unfavorably in the industrial sphere. Gold exports were frequent until midsummer. At this time, it seems that all countries drew home their capital, especially short-time loans, so that a dissolution of the international money market resulted. Political influences, too, turned the flow of funds homeward. With the upswing of business, more funds were required for production and for commerce. Stock exchanges engaged in liquidations, because of political disturbances arising out of the Balkan controversy and the German-French trouble over Morocco. Because of these conditions, business confidence was impaired and the demand for money became general, even to the point that runs were made on deposit banks in Germany, and particularly in France.[1] French banks adopted a noticeable contraction policy with regard to both home and foreign demands for credit. Both the market and bank rates rose during the later months of the year.

During the first three quarters of 1910, the London money market experienced an easing of rates, but during the last quarter it felt an ever increasing strain. This stringency was due to several causes: excessive issues of securities; much speculation in oil and rubber shares; the prosperous condition of industry and trade at home and abroad; prevalent labor difficulties; and an urgent demand for funds to move the large crops of Egypt, India, Canada and Russia. This drain was somewhat relieved by the fact that continental demands for funds were met in part by France and Holland, and Argentina's needs were taken care of by Germany. The United States, on the other hand, in view of her less favorable trade balance, liquidated European loans in order to aid the situation at home. During 1911

[1] Deposits in savings banks of Germany and France; reserves of central banks and cash holdings and time deposits of German Joint Stock banks:

	Deposits in *savings banks* (rate of increase (+) and decrease (—) over preceding year in %)		Reserves of *central banks* (In million dollars)		Cash holdings and time deposits of the *German Joint Stock Banks* (Increase (+) decrease (—) over preceding year (In million dollars)	
	Germany	*France*	*Germany*	*France*	*Cash holdings*	*Time deposits*
1908	+4.8%	+5.1%	$259	$764	+$12.2	+$71.3
1909	+7.7	+4.7	266	873	+ 16.3	+ 21.8
1910	+7.0	+3.1	268	823	+ 9.2	+ 61.6
1911	+6.2	—0.5	288	779	+ 3.7	+ 57.1
1912	+4.8	+1.4	295	778	+ 4.3	+ 32.7

the money market in England assumed a brighter aspect once more, in spite of political difficulties, brought about by the budget controversy. Internal requirements of course persisted, but foreign demand was somewhat smaller than usual. The calls for funds from Egypt and Argentina were lighter because of bad harvests. Declining interest rates in the money market of the United States enabled Europe to borrow freely there, a state of affairs extremely welcome in England, since her burden in meeting the continental demand was by so much further lightened. Activity on the bourse had been somewhat dampened by the collapse in the boom in oil and rubber shares. A large export business resulted in a more favorable trade balance, and advanced Enlgand's position as a creditor nation.

During this period, beginning with 1908, and continuing up to the middle of 1910, the United States bore a peculiar relation to the international money market, in that continental countries carried on a heavy demand for gold, and that the relative absence of new foreign loans and foreign investments in the United States was coincident with considerable liquidation of American securities held abroad. The consequent withdrawal of American funds from Europe to meet domestic needs was, in turn, followed by a cessation of European demands for gold. This, coupled with a remarkable favorable trade balance, resulted in a return flow of gold into this country. In view of the business reaction that obtained at that time, the year 1911 was characterized by a sufficiency of loanable funds, and American lenders again made their appearance abroad. European borrowing was of course particularly active during the partial dissolution of the European international money market in the fall of 1911, as previously mentioned.

Volume of Production and Trade. In the first half of 1910, the physical volume of production and trade, in the

United States, progressed in a very halting manner; and during the second half, it decidedly decreased. Subsequently, it maintained a steady volume until the fall of 1911.[1] Bank clearings outside of New York support this conclusion, and the gross earnings of railroads also give evidence that business activity followed the course described, —although the very moderate crop-yield lessened the normal seasonal volume of railroad traffic in the fall of 1910. Foreign commerce shows the influence of price levels and business activity here, as related to those abroad. Imports remained static, but the totals were somewhat larger than they were in 1909, while exports increased considerably during 1910-11. Especially was there a notable increase in exports of raw materials and manufactured articles.

Turning to particular industries for evidence as to the volume of production, we find that the U. S. Steel Corporation's unfinished orders declined, throughout 1910, to a marked degree. From 5,926,000 tons in December, 1909, the volume shrank to 2,675,000 tons in the same month of 1910. The concern gave evidence of a gradual, though halting, recovery in 1911. Up to October, the orders had increased only to 3,611,000, but by December, 1911, had jumped to 5,085,000 tons. The total production of steel in 1911 was 9.2 per cent less than in 1910, while the production in 1910 was 9 per cent greater than in 1909 and was the largest ever reported. Pig iron production, which increased remarkably during the last eight months of 1909, presents a gradual decline throughout 1910, yet reached a record volume for the year of 27,262,000 gross tons, as against 25,795,000 in 1909. After reaching a very low point during the later months of 1910, pig iron production gradually increased during 1911 to a total of 23,-650,000 gross tons for the year.

[1] *Cf. supra*, p. 43—Index Number of Production.

The coal industry manifested a striking divergence from the general course of production. In spite of the lethargy of business as a whole, there existed a good domestic and foreign demand. Production of coal increased 5 per cent for anthracite and 9 per cent for general mining in 1910, and 8 per cent and 4 per cent, respectively, in 1911. The National Coal Operators Association, organized in 1910, adopted an agressive marketing policy, and exports increased upon an unprecedented scale. The total anthracite shipments increased from 61,970,000 tons in 1910 to 69,954,000 in 1911.

In the copper industry, there was a general curtailment of production during 1910-11. Although it was estimated that consumption of copper had increased throughout the world by 10 per cent in 1910, the effect upon copper production remained nil, for a considerable surplus remained on hand to be worked off. By the time the surplus stock had nearly disappeared in 1911, the demand receded and production was necessarily restricted. There was, however, a considerable recovery in that industry during the closing months of 1911, and even though the industry was forced to limit output, the entire volume of copper produced actually exceeded the total attained in 1909.

Like the copper industry, cotton manufacturing adopted a policy of drastic curtailment of production during 1910, together with occasional reduction of prices. The reason for this policy is said to have lain in the high price of raw cotton. The continuously rising prices abroad, and the shortage of the cotton crop in 1909, stimulated demand for raw cotton, and drove the price beyond the point of profit for the domestic manufacturers, hampered as they were by a descending price level. It was estimated that the curtailment of production had proceeded in January, 1911, to the extent of 50 per cent of the total number of spindles in operation.[1] A decline in the price of raw cotton, in 1911, relieved somewhat these unfavorable conditions.

Crop production in 1910 was good. The corn and oats yields in the United States were exceptional; wheat was moderate, and the cotton yield was normal. India also produced a normal crop of cotton. The world's production of corn was abundant, while wheat crops experienced serious reverses in many countries, especially in India, France, and Argentina. In 1911, the cotton yield broke all records for the United States, with a total of 16,000,000 bales, and the return was almost as favorable in India. The corn harvests in this year were generally poor, especially in Argentina, where the crop was a complete failure; Austria-Hungary also reported a very poor yield. The wheat crop was very meager in the United States and Russia, while in the other wheat-producing countries the yield was very good.

Production of Crops

	Corn (In million bushels)			Wheat (In million bushels)			Cotton (In million bales)	
	U.S.	*Argentina*	*Austria*	*U.S.*	*Russia*	*France*	*U.S.*	*India*
1909	2,552	177	210	683	711	356	10.1	4.1
1910	2,886	175	240	635	699	257	11.6	3.6
1911	2,531	27	181	621	447	315	15.6	3.2

Total for World

	Corn	Wheat
1909	3,563	3,581
1910	4,031	3,575
1911	3,481	3,551

The Volume of Business in Europe. Indexes of the volume of production and trade give evidence of a continuous growth in 1910 in Germany, England, and France. A similar situation prevailed also in 1911, except that France as the result of the crop failure in 1910, experienced

[1] *Cf. Chronicle*, vol. xcii, p. 10.

a slight retardation in industrial expansion during the second half of 1910 and the first few months of 1911.

Statistics showing the volume of business in Germany, France and England are presented below:

GERMANY

(IN MILLION OF DOLLARS)

	Gross earnings of railroads	*Bank clearings*	*Imports*	*Exports*	*Unemployment* [1] *(In per cent)*
1909	$677	$12,235	$2,028	$1,569	2.8%
1st half		6,173			3.4
2nd half		6,062			2.2
1910	723	12,940	2,126	1,779	1.9
1st half		6,406			2.1
2nd half		6,534			1.8
1911	780	15,005	2,310	1,929	1.9
1st half		7,137			1.9
2nd half		7,868			1.8
FRANCE					
1909	344	5,620	1,205	1,104	8.1
1st half		2,800			9.8
2nd half		2,820			6.7
1910	356	6,192	1,384	1,203	6.5
1st half		3,091			7.3
2nd half		3,101			5.6
1911	369	6,721	1,557	1,164	6.2
1st half		3,406			6.0
2nd half		3,315			6.7
ENGLAND					
1909	539	65,617	2,595	1,840	7.7
1st half		32,268			8.2
2nd half		33,349			7.2
1910	556	71,333	2,796	2,094	4.7
1st half		36,298			5.0
2nd half		35,035			4.3
1911	570	71,117	2,812	2,211	3.0
1st half		36,434			3.1
2nd half		34,683			2.9

[1] For the source of the unemployment statistics, *cf. supra*, p. 48.

During 1910, the manufacturing industries were extremely prosperous in England, with the exception of cotton manufacturing, which was very slack because of the high price of raw cotton and the paucity of the supply. Coal, too, lagged a little, because of partial disorganization following strikes, so that production remained about as it was in 1909. Foreign trade exceeded, in 1910, all previous totals. During, 1911, the industrial and trade expansion continued, as did foreign trade, which made record advances again during this year. There were two exceptions in this general advance. Cotton made only a slight improvement, while coal production increased over all former figures, and the pig iron industry, which had suffered an overproduction in 1910, saw production in 1911 contracted to the 1909 level.

In Germany a similar development in production and trade took place. The textile industry lagged in 1910, as it did in England, and for the same reasons,—lack of raw material and its high price—and did not better itself until the latter part of 1911. The pig iron industry met a slight retardation in its increasing rate of production in 1911, but, on the whole, remained very prosperous. Foreign commerce increased beyond all previous figures in 1910-11. The unfavorable trade balance was less in 1910 than in 1911. Although exports of manufactured articles increased considerably in 1911, and other commodities showed an advance, these were strikingly offset by the heavy imports of foodstuffs.

What was true of England and Germany is not entirely applicable to France. Coal and pig iron production, however, was continuous, as shown in the following table:

Coal and Pig Iron Production in France

	Coal (Million long tons)	Pig Iron (Hundreds of thousands long tons)
1909	37	35
1910	38	40
1911	39	44

Bank clearings, gross earnings of railroads, and the volume of bills of exchange in circulation, evidenced an increasing volume of business. Foreign trade increased in 1910, but a greater unfavorable balance occurred toward the close of the year, as a result of the crop failure. In 1911, on the whole, exports actually declined, while imports increased, largely as a result of greater importations of foodstuffs during the first half of the year. It is estimated by the *Economiste Européen* that the vintage yield in 1910 was 47.6 per cent below normal, and that wheat production was only 257,000,000 bushels as against 356,000,000 in 1909 and 315,000,000 in 1911. The decline in exports in 1911 was entirely in foods and raw materials. Exports of manufactured articles increased moderately. The retardation of industrial expansion in France during the latter part of 1910 and the first part of 1911 was limited mainly to the agricultural sections, though industry and trade as a whole felt a slightly depressing effect.

Statistics of trade and production during 1910-11 point to the conclusion that the physical volume of business increased for England and Germany, and to some extent also for France, but that the rate of increase was somewhat retarded in the construction, building, and textile trades, during the first half of 1911. Conditions in France point to a reaction in the latter part of 1910 and the beginning of 1911, as a result of reverses in the agricultural industries. The primary factors causing this retardation in European business were as follows: first and foremost, the depression in

America, which brought about a restricted market for European products, and the growing competition of American products in European market. Second, the political disturbances, especially those arising from the Balkan trouble and the Franco-German controversy. These political factors produced considerable disturbances in the money market, leading, on the one hand, to the hoarding of specie, and the recalling of funds loaned abroad, and, on the other, to heavy demands, both public and private, for capital. Finally, the increased cost of living in continental countries produced considerable labor unrest, resulting in a greater demand for credit to meet, temporarily, the rising labor costs, as well as in a contraction of the consumers' and producers' demand. This third factor had slightly different results in France; for in order to maintain their standard of living, investors had turned, especially in 1910, away from domestic low-income-yielding, to foreign higher-income-yielding, securities, thus restricting, somewhat, the fulfillment of domestic capital requirements.

The Course of Commodity Prices. The United States witnessed the culmination of its period of rising prices in March, 1910. A gradual decline of general wholesale prices set in subsequently and continued until May, 1911, with no strong recovery until 1912.

WHOLESALE PRICES IN THE UNITED STATES—BUREAU OF LABOR STATISTICS

	1910				*1911*			
	All commodities	*Farm products*	*Raw materials*	*Mfd. articles*	*All commodities*	*Farm products*	*Raw materials*	*Mf[d.] arti[cles]*
Jan.	132.7	169.4	144.9	129.7	128.9	*155.0* [a]	136.1	127
Mar.	*133 8* [b]	*181.0* [b]	*144.9* [b]	*131.0* [b]	129.3	156.2	135.9	127
May	131.9	168.5	140.3	129.7	*128.1* [a]	157.5	*135.0* [a]	126
Sept.	131.3	159.3	138.2	129.5	129.8	168.2	141.4	126
Dec.	130.4	150.5	136.5	128.8	129.2	169.6	145.8	*125*

[a] *lowest* [b] *highest*

Compare with data of 1908 on page 23.

It is interesting to note that prices of separate groups of commodities attained their highest point simultaneously during March, 1910, following their recovery in 1908. The prices of farm products, which had made the greatest increase, fell sharply and reached bottom in December, 1910, —recovered, and advanced again throughout 1911; those of raw materials declined until November, and subsequently moved along an even level until June, 1911, when they too began to rise; while prices of manufactured articles gradually gave way and continued to do so throughout 1911.[1]

A review of the prices of particular commodities reveals the fact that prices of steel products were manipulated downwards throughout 1910-11. The greatest revisions occurred during the summer months of both years. Pig iron prices receded sharply to the extent of 20 per cent from January to September, 1910. They were held for a year from that time, as per agreement, and when the agreement among producers ended, and prices gave way under rigorous competiton, during October and November, 1911, the pig iron market became completely demoralized. The copper market labored under the pressure of large surplus stocks, and prices oscillated between 12 and 13 cents per pound throughout the two years. Cotton prices began falling from the high level they attained in the summer of 1910 (August—low 15.20; high 19.76 per lb.) and reached an average of 9.40 cents per lb. in December, 1911.

The trend of prices in Europe may be seen in English wholesale commodity prices. The sharp rise occurring in the latter half of 1909 was halted during the first part of 1910, and was then followed by another sharp advance.

[1] In this connection, it must be remarked that the Bureau of Labor Index of general wholesale prices is too heavily weighted with manufactured commodities to be of service in an accurate measurement of general prices.

Again a halting movement ensued in the beginning of 1911, and continued until July, when another advance set in which continued during the remaining months of that year. Prices advanced 9 per cent during these two years. On the continent, the rise in prices was greater in 1911 than in 1910, commensurate with the onward movement of business activity.[1]

Credit Expansion and the Demand for Capital. An analysis of the composite statements of all national banks during 1910-11 indicates a continuous expansion of loans until the spring of 1910, after which, the volume fluctuated but did not gain until November, 1910. After a sharp contraction in December, 1910, and January, 1911, as a result of the depleted bank reserves and low ebb of business activity, a slight expansion occurred. This expansion in 1911 can be attributed principally to the enlargement of loans by the New York banks. There was a mild retardation during the fall months, when reserves were again becoming low.

LOANS AND DISCOUNTS OF ALL NATIONAL BANKS AND NEW YORK CLEARING HOUSE BANKS

(IN MILLION DOLLARS)

	All National Banks Reporting dates		
	1909	*1910*	*1911*
Jan.	——	$5,264	$5,443
Feb.	$4,870	——	——
Mar.	——	5,464	5,588
Apr.	4,988	——	——
June	5,061	5,456	5,634
Sept.	5,158	5,497	5,690
Nov.	5,191	5,498	——
Dec.	——	——	5,695

	New York Clearing House Banks Average for month		
	1909	*1910*	*1911*
Jan.	$1,325	$1,202	$1,242
Mar.	1,305	1,245	1,343
June	1,352	1,199	1,366
Nov.	1,219	1,217	1,345

[1] Index number for France as given by the *Annuaire Statistique* and the *Réforme Économique*; for Germany, computed from the prices published in the *Vierteljahrshefte zur Statistik.*

The New York clearing house banks show a sharp contraction of loans during the fall of 1909, while the liquidation of the stock market was going on. After reaching the lowest point of the year in December, they maintained a constant volume throughout 1910. In January and February of 1911, a sudden expansion occurred and continued until July, when another contraction took place. This state of affairs closely follows the trend of prices and sales on the stock market. It is to be noted that the contraction in production and trade was not so great during 1910-11, and that the general price level did not decline to such a great extent. The decrease in the physical volume of production, trade and prices occurred largely during the latter part of 1910 and the early part of 1911. The loans of interior banks follow very closely the course of trade and prices in exhibiting a gradually diminishing rate of decline during 1910 and a growing rate of increase in 1911, especially during the closing months of the year.

As a result of the declining profits in industry and low interest rates, investment conditions in this country favored bonds more than stocks, until the latter part of 1911. During 1910, sales of stocks and bonds declined in volume, but bonds recovered in September and increased throughout 1911, while the volume of sales of stocks did not cease receding until August, 1911. Even then the trading in securities was not at all comparable with the volume of sales in 1908 or 1909.

Applications for investment funds, if judged by the listing of new issues on the New York stock exchange, receded in 1910, falling below the 1909 totals. Industrial stocks gained, however, while bonds and all other stocks receded. In 1911 new listings diminished for all securities to a level comparable with that of 1907 and 1908. Building operations receded in 1910, but maintained a steady volume in 1911. It is to be noted, however, that building actually increased in cities outside of New York City during the first half of 1910. New security listings, and the monthly value of building permits in 20 leading cities, were as follows:

	Stocks (In $1,000,000)	*Bonds* (In $1,000,000)
1909	$297	$713
1910	304	572
1911	256	398

Building permits (In $100,000)	*1909*	*1910*	*1911*
1st qt.	$1,403	$1,280	$1,127
2nd qt.	1,997	1,633	1,534
3rd qt.	1,583	1,273	1,596
4th qt.	1,171	1,212	1,122
Total	$6,154	$5,398	$5,379

During the latter part of 1909 and throughout 1910 there was considerable offering of short-term notes, as well as bonds, abroad. The apathy of investors in the United States was so acute during the early part of 1910 that borrowings of cities like Philadelphia, Baltimore, Chicago, and Milwaukee failed, and New York City revenue bonds sought sale abroad. This situation continued to some extent during 1911, when there was considerable listing of American securities in Berlin and Paris; but during the summer and early fall of 1911, many foreign-held securities were returned to the American market. The fear of war in Europe caused the withdrawal of bank deposits, and hoarding became extensive. These disturbances in the money market brought about security liquidation on a broad scale by financial institutions and investors.

Issues of New Securities Abroad. The emission of new securities abroad was noteworthy. In England they broke all records,—reaching a total of $1,301 millions in 1910 and $932 millions in 1911. Approximately 43 per cent in 1910 and 55 per cent in 1911 were foreign issues, while 35 per cent and 33 per cent, respectively, were issues of British possessions, and the remaining were of domestic origin. The 1910 issues were in large part rubber and oil shares, while issues of railroad bonds of the United States and South America, and of industrial stocks generally were also very large. Capital issues in France broke previous records in 1910, when a total of $1,122 millions was brought forth. These also were mainly foreign, this class totalling $945 millions; of that amount $340 millions were government loans, as compared with $162 millions in 1909. Of the remaining amount, transportation securities increased, while industrials receded. In 1911, security issues still continued heavy, especially in the first half of the year, a total of $922 millions being floated. Foreign government applications again bulked large, with a total of $197 millions. Among all foreign issues, the South American were largest. The domestic industrials also gained in 1911. In Germany the new security issues, although large, were not as heavy as those in other countries. Emissions of public and private securities reached $644 millions in 1910, and $570 millions in 1911. This was below the record of 1908, when the total was swelled by large governmental loans—as was also true in 1909. Foreign and domestic private issues reached their largest volume in 1911, though they had maintained themselves at a high level during the two preceding years. Emissions of domestic industrial stocks attained their highest volume in 1910. It may be seen from what has been said, how enormous were the capital demands existing during these years. A large amount of foreign securities, floated upon European investment markets, were paid for by commodities; since England, France and Germany maintained a positive gold balance without interruption during this period of heavy foreign capital issues.

Gold and Trade Balance of Germany, France, England and United States
(in million dollars)

	United States Gold	United States Trade	Germany Gold	Germany Trade	France Gold	France Trade	England Gold	England Trade
1908	—$31	+$637	+$74	—$301	+$192	—$114	—$19	—$663
1909	— 89	+ 225	+ 7	— 459	+ 35	— 101	+ 36	— 755
1910	— 00.4	+ 266	+ 42	— 347	+ 11	— 181	+ 31	— 702
1911	+ 20	+ 525	+ 35	— 381	+ 24	— 393	+ 42	— 601

In connection with these heavy demands for capital, we find favorable conditions in the increased deposits in the savings banks of England and Germany. Cash reserve holdings of the Bank of England and of the Joint Stock banks increased also, as did those of the Reichsbank. On the other hand, deposits in savings banks in France decreased from 1910 to 1911, as did also the reserve of gold and silver of the Bank of France. It became a noticeable fact in 1910, that French capital was seeking investment abroad, in the higher income-yielding securities. This was also true to a smaller extent in 1911.[1]

In addition to these heavy applications for capital, there occurred an expansion in commercial loans by the banks of Europe, to meet the needs of business, because of the continuous growth in the physical volume of production and trade and rising prices. Loanable funds seemed ample, for the large quantities of gold garnered by continental banks in 1908 especially, now served their purpose well in meeting both commercial and investment demands. Evidently, the United States had failed in bargaining for gold in 1908-09, when it was forced to export heavily,—a circumstance which was one of the primary causes of the depression. Later, toward the latter part of 1910 when the gold tide belatedly turned, the depression had already gotten under way.

[1] *Cf. Volkswirtschaftliche Chronik*, 1911, p. 885.

CHAPTER IV

Causes of the Depression of 1910-11

Nature of the Problem. Business depressions occur when the supply of bank credit has become exhausted. It is elastic bank credit that is the significant factor in any study of cyclical fluctuations in business conditions, that is, the varying amount of banking funds present at any given time in the cycle. It is evident, from statistical data, that money in hand-to-hand circulation does not vary greatly in volume, but that deposit currency does. Prices and production oscillate necessarily within the limits of elasticity of bank credit. When the supply of elastic bank credit reaches its upper limit, there ensues that check upon rising prices, upon increasing production, and upon growing purchasing power, which marks the culmination of a period of prosperity and the beginning of a depression. Conversely, the thing that makes possible an expansion in business activity is the presence of a supply of elastic bank credit.

The supply available at any time consists of the amount of cash reserves held by banks within a given country, and the supply of credit obtainable in foreign countries,—that supply of course being dependent upon the effectiveness of the international financial organization, that is, the facility with which credit may be obtained abroad. This factor, at any rate, limits the amount of purchasing power that can be commanded by the business world. A second variable affecting the amount of elastic bank credit available for business use at any time is to be found in the presence or absence of popular confidence in the monetary and credit systems.[1]

[1] This factor was clearly present in the causes of the panic of 1893, *cf.* W. J. Lauck, *Causes of Panic of 1893.*

In addition to the quantity of lawful reserves that banks can mobilize out of the available supply of legal tender at hand in a country, and of credits obtainable abroad, there is a second determinant of business depressions. When bank credit is unequally distributed or disproportionately used, purchasing power becomes unsteady, the price system is deranged and the production system is subject to maladjustments;— all of which hastens curtailment in the growth of business actiivty. The moment at which this disproportionately used supply of elastic bank credit becomes depleted is determined in great measure by a third factor, namely, the degree of intensity of business activity. Business activity, of course is animated primarily by prospective margins of profit. These margins in turn are conditioned by present indications of the future trend of costs and selling prices and the probable volume of business to be expected. Elastic bank credit, accordingly, may be used more or less rapidly by the business world. A more rapid use of purchasing power would involve of course innumerable factors which exert a propitious influence upon business profits. The first step in the progress of a period of depression is taken when high interest rates, as a result of depleted bank reserves, begin to restrict the expansion of business activity, during a period of cumulation of prosperity. This restricting force deranges the price system, throws into bold relief the maladjustments in production, checks the even flow of goods through the productive process, accentuates the evidence of unequal distribution of purchasing power,— and the liquidation process is ushered in.

Let us now endeavor to analyze the business data presented in the preceding chapters with a view to determining what, exactly, were the causes of the business depression of 1910-11. First, let us consider the amount of bank funds that were available for American business, especially from the standpoint of those factors which operated to reduce the supply during 1908-09. Second, let us study the effects produced by the disproportionate use of funds during 1908-09. Such an analysis, to be sure, can be extended only to certain general investment categories, such as security trading, commodity trading, and production, since a closer study is too difficult for the amount of data that is obtainable. Third, let us attempt to estimate the degree of intensity of business activity in 1908-09, our preliminary object being to determine whether American business experienced greater difficulties, during 1908-09, in procuring the necessary funds for carrying on, than it did during the preceding boom period of 1904-07; and whether the cumulation of financial strain was more rapid in 1908-09 than it was during the earlier period.

The Supply of Funds in 1908. In its wider aspects, the question of the supply of funds available for business use involves such factors as accumulated capital, various savings, shifting of foreign loans, gold movements, money in circulation, and bank credit,—the volume of the latter conditioned by the rapidity and smoothness of the flow of goods through the economic process,—even the supply of merchantile credit, and banking efficiency and economy in the use of exchange media. To measure all of these relevant factors, especially for the purpose of making comparisons among different periods, would be extremely difficult. Hence it is not easy to establish the fact that the supply of loanable funds in the United States, during 1908, was insufficient to carry forward the business revival into an extended period of prosperity.[1] However, since the varying supply of elastic bank credit is after all the most significant element in supply of funds, it may well serve as the focus of our attention in studying the causes of the business depression under consideration. We shall, there-

[1] *Cf. supra*, pp. 19-21.

fore, take—as proper criteria for a comparison of the supply of funds available—interest rates and reserve holdings of banks during the last half of 1908 and of 1904, respectively,—these two periods corresponding to the beginning of the respective business revivals.

In August 1908, the average call-loan rate for the month in New York stood at 1.06 per cent; and 60-90 day paper, although it showed an average for the month of only 3.61 per cent, continued to decline. If these rates are compared with those prevailing in 1904, no marked difference is noticeable; for call loan rates stood at .90 per cent for August, of that year, and 60-90 day paper reached its lowest point in July, 3.55 per cent.[1] Bank reserves further illustrate the easy condition of the credit market in 1908. The New York clearing house banks in August, 1908, show an average reserve ratio of 29.69 per cent which had progressively increased from 21.84 per cent in December 1907. During June the total amount of surplus reserves stood at $68,233,025, the largest in fourteen years. On May 14, 1908, the ratio of cash reserves of all National banks to the net deposits was 18.6 per cent, the highest ratio for the year, while their cash holdings increased from $791 millions, on February 14, to $871 millions on September 23, the highest figure ever reported by these banks. If these reserves are compared with those of 1904, a small degree of difference will be noted. The average reserves of the New York banks for August, 1904, was 29.61 per cent, while on June 9, 1904, the ratio of cash reserves of all National banks to their net deposits was 18.1 per cent; these were the highest figures for the year. If we compare average reserve ratios of New York clearing-house banks

[1] An even tolerably scientific basis is lacking before the year 1904 for comparing the amounts of loanable funds present during various periods of business depression. The monetary system underwent considerable change up to 1900.

during the two entire periods of depression, namely from November, 1902, to July, 1904, and from January to September, 1908, the figures stand at 26.76 per cent for the former and 28.44 per cent for the latter. We conclude of course, from this comparison, that the supply of banking funds was greater in 1908 than it was in 1902-04.

With this potential supply of bank credit at hand in America, European loan funds played no great part in our credit market during 1908, though Europe was in a position to loan. There was a strong movement on the part of continental countries toward acquiring gold reserves. This tendency, in connection with the rather high interest rates prevailing there, and together with the return to those countries of funds loaned broad, because of the universal business depression, netted for Europe a rather sizable increase in gold.[1] Nevertheless, American business had become accustomed to borrowing abroad, and the impression remained that funds would be forthcoming if required.

The Retarded Growth of Banking Funds in 1908-09. Of crucial significance to the problem is the failure of loanable funds to increase normally during the period of business revival and cumulative prosperity, from the last half of 1908 until the close of 1909. This failure of banking resources to expand in proper ratio to prosperity was due to the fact that the net gain in our stock of gold, in 1908, from foreign and domestic sources combined, was $49 millions, and that the net loss in 1909 was $16 millions, leaving the net gain for the two years only $33 millions. Such net

[1] Expert opinion indicates that Europe recalled her funds in 1907 and thereafter. *Cf.* Prof. Levis, *Review of Reviews*, vol. xxxvii, p. 98; *cf.* O. M. W. Sprague, *Economic Journal*, vol. xviii, pp. 353-72; *cf. Moody's Magazine*, vol. xi, pp. 45-51. Moody estimates that up to May 1, 1906, we had borrowed from Europe $450 millions. O. M. W. Sprague estmates that we borrowed $100 millions in gold in 1906 alone. This produced a very untenable basis for our credit system in following years. *Cf. supra*, p. 22.

loss of gold as that which occurred in 1909 had not been known since 1895. Compared with the previous period of business expansion, from 1904 to 1907, this difference in the gold situation looms large; for during those four years the total net gain was $398 millions. This lack of growth in the gold supply was reflected in sluggish increases in the monetary stock of the United States. During the fiscal years 1904 to 1907, the total stock gained 16.5 per cent, while from 1908 to 1909 it gained only 8 per cent. The proportional distribution of the total monetary stock, however, between the public and the banks, grew in favor of the banks. In 1905, leaving out the amount held by the federal treasury, the proportion stood: banks 42.5 per cent —public 57.5 per cent. In 1907 the relation stood 41.1 per cent to 58.9 per cent; in 1908, banks 45.9 per cent—public 54.1 per cent; in 1909, banks 47.3 per cent—public 52.7 per cent.[1] But this concentration of monetary stock in the hands of the banks, accomplished chiefly by the substitution of deposit currency for the use of money, could not materially offset the subnormal accretion of gold stock on bank reserves. Cash holdings of all National banks in 1909 increased only 1.7 per cent over those held in 1908, while the increase from 1904 to 1907 was 6.7 per cent. There was, moreover, a greater expansion in business activity in 1908 than there was in the latter period. The greatest increase in these reserves occurred between 1907 and 1908, when it reached 23.7 per cent. This disproportionately large increase was the result of strenuous efforts to increase the gold supply during the panic days of 1907. It left its impress on the credit situation, for it gave rise, together with the prevailing business depres-

[1] Figures taken from Mitchell, *op. cit.*, p. 296. Because of the inelasticity of the National Bank note system this proportional increase in favor of the banks was smaller than it otherwise would have been.

sion, to cheap credit in 1908, and in conjunction with other influences, fostered an outflow of gold to foreign countries. The net outflow was almost continuous, and from April, 1908 to February, 1910, amounted to $123,765,000. With such a slow accumulation of reserves and this almost stationary volume of monetary stock in the United States, the possibility of supplying bank credit in 1908-09 was necessarily limited.

As we shall see in later pages, the abnormal accretion of gold in 1906-07 stimulated investment operations, because of the cheap price of credit. But this very activity produced a critical situation, for the gold supply, which should have acted as the basis for further credit operations was being withdrawn by heavy exportations, especially in 1909.

We may draw, therefore, a provisional conclusion, namely, that the supply of bank credit could not keep pace with the accumulating demand for funds and that the business expansion stimulated partly by the huge gold accretions of 1906-07 could not be sustained. Although the supply of bank funds was plentiful in 1908, the reserve position of the banking community was weakened by heavy exportations of gold.

The Use and Distribution of Funds in 1908-09. Very early in 1908, bank funds were in urgent demand in the security market, as is evidenced by an analysis of investment data. This activity, stimulated by low rates on call money increased until September, 1909. In that short period, prices of securities as well as volume of sales showed considerable advance. The average prices of twenty railroad stocks, which we may assume to furnish a criterion, rose from 88.8 in February, 1908 to 131.6 in August, 1909, the increase during these nineteen months being 48.2 per cent.[1] From October, 1903, to January,

[1] *Cf. supra*, p. 16. Babson's computation of 32 selected stocks gives

1906, or twenty-eight months of the previous boom period, the increase had been 48.3 per cent. The average price of twelve industrial stocks during the former period increased 38.8 per cent, as compared with a 78.5 per cent increase during the latter period. Nor must we overlook the volume of stock sales, if we would gain a proper comparative estimate of the extent to which speculative activity employed funds in these two periods. The number of shares of stock sold on the New York stock exchange increased from 39,650,000 during the last quarter of 1907, to 58,070,000 in the last quarter of 1909, while the volume increased from 32,490,000 during the first quarter of 1904 to 79,680,000 in the first quarter of 1906. The increase, therefore, was 46.5 per cent during the two years of 1908 and 1909, as compared with 145.5 per cent during the two years of 1904 and 1906. It must be remembered that the volume of stock sales continued large throughout 1906, though the first serious break in the stock market did not occur until March, 1907.

If we turn to the estimates of security issues for new capital during 1908 and 1909, a strong spirit of investment enterprise becomes manifest. New issues of stock listed on the New York stock exchange fell somewhat into abeyance during 1908 with a total of $124 millions, but this increased to $297 millions in 1909. This was the largest yearly stock issue listed since the boom years of 1899 and 1901. In 1904, 1905, and 1906, the listings were $121, $125, and $237 millions, respectively. New bond issues listed totalled $649 millions par value in 1908 and $713 millions in 1909, thereby breaking all previous records. The total of bond issues listed during the three years of 1904-06 was $1302 millions as compared with $1362 millions during the two years of 1908-09.

supporting evidence of a similar rise in other securities. Their average increase was approximately from 70 to 120 from December, 1907, to August, 1909.

This data leads us to the conclusion that the rise in prices of securities was somewhat greater during the period 1904-07 than it was in 1908-09, (though the advance in railroad stocks was nearly equal). The greatest difference between these two periods lies in the volume of stock sales. These were extraordinarily large in 1904-06. When, however, new security issues are compared by means of the only dependable data offered,—listings upon the New York stock exchange,—it becomes evident that the flotation of new securities in 1908-09 exceeded by far that of the much longer period 1904-07.

The trend of loan and discount volumes of the New York clearing house banks corresponds in growth with fairly rapid developments in the security market. The first item stood at an average of $1,129,200,000 for January, 1908, and increased to $1,356,900,000 for August, 1909—the months when the security market began its decline. By November, 1909, loans and discounts of these banks had declined to $1,218,000,000. Net deposits for January 1908 were $1,091 millions, for August 1909 $1,416 millions and for November 1909, $1,205 millions. The cash reserves were reduced from an average of $407,000,000 in August, 1908, to $301,000,000 in December, 1909. The reserve ratio stood at 29.61 per cent, the average for August, 1908, but declined to 26.57 per cent in the succeeding twelve months and by November, 1909, had reached 25.54 per cent, a bare surplus over the legal minimum. The expansion in loans for these banks had occurred chiefly before October, 1908, and they maintained a very nearly equal volume until August, 1909, upon a basis of reserves only slightly above the legal limit. During the first phase of loan expansion, the price of credit remained relatively cheap and continued so until June, 1909. In the following three months interest rates rose steadily and by October, 1909, they had advanced sharply and, with the exception of a temporary relaxation during the earlier part of 1910 remained high until the close of that year. It is evident, therefore, that bank credit for security trading had been stretched to the limit by the fall of 1909.

In comparing the intensity of activity in security trading with the corresponding utilization of banking funds for the two boom periods of 1904-07 and 1908-09, the following table is presented by way of a summary:

RELATIVE FIGURES — 1903 = 100

	Price of 12 Industrial Stocks	*Price of 20 Railroad Stocks*	*Volume of Security Sales on N. Y. Stock Exchange*		*New Listings on N. Y. Stock Exchange*	
			No. of Shares	*Par Value of Bonds*	*Stocks*	*Bonds*
1903	100	100	100	100	100	100
(4th qr.) Min.	80	92	—	—	—	—
1904	97	100	116	148	70	224
1905	142	122	163	119	72	296
1906	168	128	176	89	137	159
(1st qr.) Max.	174	(4th qr.) 130	—	—	—	—
1907	137	100	121	67	91	128
(4th qr.) Min.	106	86	—	—	—	—
1908	133	99	121	146	71	338
1909	165	122	133	187	171	371
(4th qr.) Max.	176	(3d qr.) 127	—	—	—	—

ITEMS IN STATEMENTS OF NEW YORK CLEARING HOUSE BANKS

	Loans and Discounts	*Net Deposits*	*Reserves*	*Reserve Ratio Per Cent*
1903	100	100	100	26.32
(4th qr.) Min.	98	96	96	—
1904	117	125	130	27.43
(3rd qr.) Max.	122	134	146	—
1905	120	125	122	25.87
(4th qr.) Min.	113	113	109	—
1906	115	114	111	25.68
1907	122	117	111	24.89
(4th qr.) Min.	127	118	99	—
1908	136	144	155	28.04
(4th qr.)	146	155	(3rd qr.) = 170	—
1909	144	150	149	26.14
(3rd qr.) Max.	149	156	(4th qr.) = 131	(4th qr.) = 25.74

ANALYSIS OF THE ABOVE TABLES SHOWS THE FOLLOWING RESULTS:

Index	*Period from minimum to maximum*	*Increase*	*Period from minimum to maximum*	*Increase*	*Greater + or less — in per cent of 1904–07 period over that of 1908–09*
Price of 12 Industrial Stocks	4th quarter of 1903 to 1st quarter of 1906—27 mos.	94%	4th quarter of 1907 to 4th quarter of 1909—24 mos.	70%	+24%
Price of 20 Railroad Stocks	4th quarter of 1903 to 4th quarter of 1906—36 mos.	38%	4th quarter of 1907 to 3rd quarter of 1909—21 mos.	41%	— 3%
Volume of security sales	1903–06 (3 years)	76%	1908–09 (1 year)	12%	+64%
Stocks: Bonds:	1904–06 (2 years)	59% (Decrease)	1907–09 (2 years)	120%	—61%
New listings: Stocks:	1904–06 (2 years)	67%	1908–09 (1 year)	100%	—33%
Bonds:	1903–05 (2 years)	196%	1907–09 (2 years)	243%	—47%
Loans and Discounts	4th quarter of 1903 to 3rd quarter of 1904—9 mos.	24%	4th quarter of 1907 to 4th quarter of 1908—12 mos.	19%	+ 5%
Net Deposits	4th quarter of 1903 to 3rd quarter of 1904—9 mos.	38%	4th quarter of 1907 to 4th quarter of 1908—12 mos.	37%	0
Reserves	4th quarter of 1903 to 3rd quarter of 1904—9 mos.	50%	4th quarter of 1907 to 3rd quarter of 1908—9 mos.	71%	—21%
Reserves	[illegible]d quarter of 1904 to 4th quarter of 1905—15 mos.	37% (Decrease)	3rd quarter of 1908 to 3rd quarter of 1909—12 mos.	39% (Decrease)	— 2%

Analyzing the above table one may draw the following conclusions: 1. Prices of industrial stocks rose more in 1904-06 than in 1907-09, while those of railroad stocks rose more in the latter period. 2. The volume of stock sales on the New York stock exchange increased much more in 1904-

06 than in 1908-09, but the reverse is true of bonds. 3. New security issues were considerably greater in 1908-09 than in 1904-06. 4. The banking situations, as depicted by the items in the statements of New York clearing-house banks, agree closely for the two periods. In the months of greatest expansion of loans and deposits, from the minimum to the maximum, which was 9 months in 1903-04 and 12 months in 1907-08, the relative increase was nearly the same. In fact, the increase in net deposits was identical. Cash reserves show a much greater increase during the first nine months of the period of 1907-08 than they did during a similar period in 1903-04. This increase, as previously explained, was due to the heavy imports of gold during the panic days of 1907. The decline in amount of reserves, subsequently, was brought about more rapidly in the former period, than it was in the latter.

It is evident that the use of banking funds for purposes of security trading was proceeding at a rapid rate before the revival in trade and industry had gotten under way.[1] As has been pointed out in the previous chapters, the influences that stimulated increase in the physical volume of business and rise in the general price level were already at work during the latter half of 1908. Good crops, increasing railroad earnings, and growing construction activity, these three great spheres of influence in business life, gave impetus toward increasingly properous conditions in industrial and trade circles. Imports and exports, also, expanded in volume. With production on the increase, here and there, at the close of 1908, and the fillip given to prices, demand for bank credit became noticeable in an increase in loans and discounts of all national banks. After the first few months of 1909 were past, there occurred a number of favorable circumstances, calculated to further stimulate

[1] *Cf. supra*, pp. 15-17.

business activity.[1] There came a pronounced growth in production; a new tariff act, with higher duties, was confidently expected; there was a heavy floatation of securities; a favorable agricultural outlook was coupled with a phenomenal rise in prices of farm products and materials for industries, and labor increased in efficiency. To carry on this rapidly expanding production, the demand for bank credit increased enormously, and prices swerved upward. A comparison of the growth of production and trade in 1908-09 with that of the period 1904-07 reveals the unusual rapidity of the progress in the former period.

	Relative Figures — 1903 = 100				1911-13 = 100	
	Bank Clearings outside New York	*Pig Iron Production*	*Building Permits*	*Imports*	*Stewart's Index No. of Production*	*Bureau of Labor Statistics Prices*
1903	100	100	100	100	75	86
1904	102	93	116	104	80	87
1905	106	129	160	118	86	87
1906	128	143	170	133	91	90
1907	134	146	160	143	89	95
1908	123	90	135	112	84	92
1909	144	146	196	150	94	98

ANALYSIS OF THE TABLE ABOVE GIVES THE FOLLOWING RESULTS:

1904 *1st half*		*1903 2d half*	*1904 1st half*	
Minimum	100	100	100	100
1907 *1st half*				
Maximum	124	166	173	147
Increase	24%—3 yrs.	66%—3 yrs.	73%—2½ yrs.	47%—3 yrs.
1908 *1st half*				
Minimum.	121	85	104	103
1909 *2d half*				
Maximum	155	190	192	149
		1st half	*2d half*	
Increase	34%—1½ yrs.	105%—1½ yrs.	88%—1 yr.	46%—1 yr.

[1] This cautious restraint of business activity in the forepart of 1909 was imputed also to the price-cutting program of the steel industry. *Cf. Chronicle*, vol. lxxxvii, p. 5 and *supra*, p. 50.

RELATIVE FIGURES — 1890-99 = 100

Items in Statements of All National Banks

	Loans and Discounts	Individual Deposits	Cash Reserves	Per Cent Reserve Ratio	Wholesale Commodity Prices U. S. Bureau of Labor Statistics
1904	178	192	171	17.6	113.0—Oct. 111.8 minimum
1905	192	215	174	16.4	115.9
1906	207	233	171	15.3	122.9
1907	225	240	182	15.3	129.5—Oct. 131.0 maximum
1908	246	249	226	17.8	122.8—Aug. 121.4 minimum
1909	264	277	230	16.3	126.5—Dec. 132.2 maximum
1910	—	—	—	—	131.6—Mar. 133.8 maximum

3 yrs.—Oct. 1904 to
Oct. 1907 increase = 20.8%
1⅓ yrs.—Aug. 1908 to
Dec. 1909 increase = 10.8%

These selective statistics, and the conclusions which they point, closely represent the relative conditions prevailing during these two periods. They agree with many studies which have been published, of more detailed monthly data, from which the secular and seasonal trends have been eliminated.[1] If the comparative lengths of the periods are taken into consideration, the difference in the growth of business activity becomes even more accentuated. If we measure the difference between the minimum and maximum months of each period, we find that prices rose comparatively much more in the 16 months of 1908-09 than they did in the 36 months of 1904-07, the absolute increase in the former period being one-half of the rise in the latter.

When we turn our attention to a comparison of the use of bank credit by business generally, during the two periods, we find that the only data available are furnished by the combined statement of all national banks. Let us bear in mind in this connection that loan expansion was greater in the one year from 1908-09 than the average expansion in loans

[1] Data referred to are those of the *Review of Economic Statistics* for 1919.

for the three years of 1904-07; that, in fact, it equalled the increase form 1906-07, which year saw the heaviest use of bank credit during that period. Deposits, too, increased far more rapidly in 1908-09 than in 1904-07. A different relation is evident in regard to the growth of the cash reserves, which were almost equal during the two periods. From 1907 to 1908, cash reserves increased suddenly and strikingly, due to abnormal circumstances accounted for in the reserve figures, namely the abnormal increase of gold during the panic period of 1907 an the heavy acquisitions of gold in 1906. That is to say, that, whereas the total cash reserves increased 11 per cent from 1904 to 1907, they jumped 44 per cent from 1907 to 1908, registering a rise of only 4 per cent in the following year.[1] This factor explains to some extent also the fact that loans, during 1907-08, show a greater increase than do deposits.

Because of the paucity of data upon which to base conclusions regarding the distribution of funds obtained by bank credit, our acquaintance with this element must remain, at the most general and incomplete. It is evident that a large volume of bank credit was used in security trading, old and new. Although funds, procured upon the floatation of new securities in exceptionally large amounts, were applied to construction and to the replenishment of, and addition to, working capital, nevertheless these investment operations took place without awaiting the pressure of the consumer's demand for goods. The large investment commitments of 1908, which continued strong in 1909, not only draw heavily upon bank credit, but made their influence felt in the commodity market in 1909. This opinion is supported by the sharp rise in the prices of farm

[1] These figures are not contradictory to those on page 85, for the figures given here represent the difference between the relative figures on a 1890-99 base.

products and raw materials in 1909 and the somewhat abnormal delay in the rise in prices of manufactured articles. The greater increase in imports as compared with that of exports in 1909, due to the business depression in Europe during the first half of the year, indicates that foreign demand for goods had but slight influence on business progress here. In spite of the fact that the agricultural classes, having enjoyed a good crop yield in 1908 at relatively low prices, met, in 1909, with a harvest somewhat below normal, especially in such important crops as corn and cotton, nevertheless, the exorbitant prices of farm products,—caused partly by the higher prices in foodstuffs the world over,—made good the shortage in quantity, and the purchasing power of these classes received a considerable impetus. The wage-earning classes on the other hand, still remained in an unfavorable position during the first half of 1909, since in spite of greater employment, wage cuts still prevailed. But during the last half of the year wage increases became general and unemployment was reduced to the minimum. With the greater diffusion of purchasing power and the resulting strong increase in prices of consumer's and manufactured goods, beginning in the summer of 1909, the profits of industry greatly increased. As a result, wages, the costs of materials, and interest rates rose sharply during the latter half of 1909.

From the foregoing, it may be seen that nothing unusual occurred in the way of a business boom, and that, although funds, at the beginning of the period, failed to find a proportional distribution, flowing largely into speculative and promotive enterprises, they attained a more equal distribution, during the latter half of 1909. Augmented purchasing power, flowing into the hands of the consumers, stimulated the demand for consumers' goods, in spite of the fact that the high costs of living absorbed larger portions of incomes than before. Thus was laid the basis for a continued upward swing of business activity, in the greater use of funds by business concerns through a heavier discounting of the future. This buoyant progress would have continued, in spite of serious maladjustments already present in the production and price system, had not unpropitious financial events retarded it.

Cumulation of Financial Strain. Rapid business expansion and untoward influences operating to limit the supply of loanable funds at the close of 1909 seem to have brought about a premature exhaustion of bank credit and cumulation of the financial strain. During the last half of the year, from July to December, a sudden rise in interest rates went hand in hand with progressive reduction in bank reserves and growing tension in a non-resilient credit market. The surplus reserves of New York clearing-house banks declined rapidly from July to November. The reserve ratio fell from 26.77 per cent to 25.54 per cent; and loans contracted from $1,349 to $1,192 millions and deposits declined from $1,425 to $1,170 millions. In the reports of all National banks, also, from June to November, a loss of cash was noticeable, while loans and deposits gained $130 and $222 millions respectively. The reserve ratio of all National banks dropped from 18.1 per cent to 15.1 per cent during this period. The reserve ratios of all banks remained low throughout 1910. The culmination of the activity in the security market was, as usual, the first effect of the financial strain. The effect in the commodity market was not evidenced until March, 1910, when the decline in general wholesale prices set in. Cotton and copper and related commodities were the first to feel the disturbance and drop in the market, in the fall of 1909. Because of the gradual manner in which the liquidation process took hold of business affairs, production receded without any such sudden cessation of industrial activity as had occurred in 1907.

The causes of the business depression of 1910 fall into two main groups. The first of these comprise the remote or predisposing causes, originating in business and investment enterprise. This enterprise manifested itself in general to a more marked degree in 1908-09 than in 1904-07, especially when we take into account the shorter period involved. The greater volume of new securities issued in 1908-09, as compared with that in the former period, is indicative of this expansion in investment operations. Though dealings on the stock exchange show a smaller volume of stocks; bonds, on the other hand, were dealt in to an enormous extent. To be sure, these heavy issues were made up largely of those bonds that had not found a market in 1907, and were now unloaded in an easy credit market. Much working capital, lost during the panic of 1907, was being replenished by this means. Furthermore, current construction operations were also under way. These operations demanded credit. With this strong spirit of investment enterprise, two additional factors combined to increase the demand for banking funds. The first of these was the rapid rise in the price of all materials for industries with the exception of minerals. This rise occurred principally because of underproduction in these commodities rather than because of a greater use of credit in trading in these products, or because of any abnormal demand for them. This rapid rise in the prices of farm, animal, and forestry products was also true of Europe. Industrial development seems to have overreached itself, in comparison with agricultural production. The second factor, involved with the rapid growth of production, which carried with it an increase in the utilization of credit resources, was the bringing into practical operation of all the industrial equipment and business undertakings developed during the great promotion period of 1904-07.

These circumstances, as may be seen, could not but bring about an early exhaustion of bank credit.

In conjunction with this first group, there were additional reasons for a state of depletion in credit, in the shape of certain special demands for funds in the investment market, in the fall of 1909. The foremost of these came from the interior, for the harvesting and moving of crops. This reduced bank funds in New York. A second demand came about because of the large volume of imports maintained throughout the year, as a result of the discrepancy between the rising price level in this country and the still declining price level abroad. Imports were especially heavy directly preceding the high tariff effective in August 1909. This stage of affairs had led to the drawing of a large volume of finance bills during the spring and early summer, with the hope that these obligations would be met abroad from the proceeds of cotton and grain exports in the fall. But the rather moderate harvests, together with good crops abroad, restricted these exports, and, of course, the corresponding credits were reduced below expectations. Thirdly, the selling of American securities upon foreign account, which had been persistent throughout the year, increased during the early fall months, when security prices were approaching their zenith. The result of this succession of circumstances was a sharp rise in foreign exchange rates.

A detailed scrutiny of business conditions abroad, and especially a consideration of foreign demand for funds, shows us, toward the close of 1909, a state of business revival and of growing prosperity. In Germany, England and France, production was already active, and the bourses had become animated even in the forepart of 1909, while during the latter half of the year, stocks and bonds rose in price, and prices of commodities began their upward trend. Large issues of new securities in these countries, during the year, bore heavily upon the investment market. Investments in the issues of colonial and newly developed regions, made for the purpose of obtaining new sources of raw materials and markets for manufactured articles also assumed greater proportions.

This expansion of industry in foreign fields, together with the above cited demand for capital from colonial and economically backward countries, as well as from domestic sources, resulted in a great application for funds in European credit markets. On the other hand, reduction in the volume of loans among European investment markets, because of political apprehensions arising out of the Balkan upheaval and other European and Asia Minor disturbances, tended to reduce the supply of available funds.

Let us now consider the second group—the immediate causes that halted the business expansion in the beginning of 1910. Credit is the medium by which business activity is buoyed up and intensified, as ships of trade are borne upon the waves of the sea. Business cycles are the credit waves, so to speak, upon which prices and production rise and fall.

Supply of credit determines the limit to which business activity may be carried forward. But the rapidity with which this limit is reached is determined by the degree of use of credit, itself determined by the variable business enterprise,—that force which affects the rise and fall of prices through the use of credit, and is thereby affected, reacting again upon the use of credit and finally upon the supply itself.

As we have previously observed, the sudden and marked increase of bank reserves in the year 1907-08 was due to the large importation of gold in 1906-07. This increase, in conjunction with the business depression, led to low interest rates. This condition fostered security trading, investment operations and commodity trading, and later in 1909, when prices rose because of the increasing use of purchasing power, swelled production. Business revival, therefore, was transformed into cumulative prosperity, in the latter half of 1909. But the supply of gold, upon which these credit operations had been built, did not remain intact for American business. The net outflow, as we have seen, was almost continuous from April, 1908, to February, 1910, amounting during that period to $123,765,000. This loss of gold was reflected in a retardation in the growth of bank reserves, and in an almost stationary volume of monetary stock in the United States from 1908 to 1909. The reserve ratio of all National banks had declined continuously since 1895-96. It reached its lowest point in 1907. Thereafter, the heavy importations of gold caused a temporary increase, but, in the latter part of 1909, it again resumed the low level of 1907. This condition can be attributed only to loss of gold, since it was the only variable element in our monetary system at the time. Its result was, of course, an insufficient basis of credit for the business expansion under way. It will be remembered that the exportation of gold was brought about by the decreasing export balance of merchandise, and the recall of capital by Europe through the sale of securities and the liquidation of short term loans. This retarded growth in the export balance was the result chiefly of the diminishing surplus of agricultural products.

With this withdrawal of commercial and investment funds by Europe, came its refusal to absorb new American borrowings.[1] American issues met with strong competi-

[1] *Cf. Chronicle*, vol. xci, p. 1387, quotes the following failures of loans of municipal governments at the close of 1909:

Philadelphia	$8,000,000	4%
Baltimore	2,400,000	4%
Milwaukee	525,000	4%

Also those of Chicago and Portland.

tion in the higher-income-yielding foreign and colonial issues in the European investment markets. Demands for capital in Europe, both domestic and foreign, especially those of colonial origin, absorbed most of the floating funds.[1] It seems highly probable that European funds were being applied more and more to investments in colonial and backward countries for the purpose of developing sources of foodstuffs and raw materials as well as meeting the capital requirements of former investments in those fields. Countries outside of Europe, generallly, sought gold to bolster up their credit systems. This fact, plus the necessity of obtaining gold to meet the credit demands, and the political apprehensions that prevailed, led to a scramble for gold on the part of the central banks of Europe.

Summary of Conclusions.

1. The heavy imports of gold in 1906-07 increased the cash reserves of banks markedly in 1908, and upon these reserves was based, temporarily, the cheap credit that unduly stimulated investment and credit operations.

2. Gold and funds were at the same time suddenly withdrawn from this country by Europe. The avenues by which this was accomplished were: heavy imports of commodities; selling of securities; and the recall of loan funds. The diminishing surplus of farm products for export aided the process.

3. The inelastic credit system provided no resiliency in banking funds during the period of financial strain. The former dependency of American business upon Europe for funds in times of stress was not possible. The various

[1] *Cf. Volkswirtschaftliche Chronik*, vol. 1909, pp. 958 *et seq.*; *cf. infra*, p. 170. See note on the proportion of foreign security issues in the English market. For example, of the $729 millions of new securities admitted on the Paris Bourse in 1909, $466 millions were foreign.

drains upon the European investment markets closed them, in large part, against American demands for funds.

4. Heavy investment operations, initial operations of concerns promoted before 1907, plus the underproduction in farm products and active speculation caused high prices for materials and foodstuffs,—all of which demanded more credit.

5. The degree of business activity in industrial and trade circles was greater in 1908-09 than in 1904-07, while it also manifested itself strongly in the investment fields. This led to a rapid utilization of credit resources.

CHAPTER V

THE RETURN OF PROSPERITY IN 1912

The General Nature of the Revival. During the gradual retrogression of business in the United States in 1910 and most of 1911,—a movement in which liquidation took place without financial disruption, in spite of high interest rates,—we find, contrary to the conditions which obtained in the depression of 1908, a gradual readjustment of production and prices to a reasonably unchanging demand; so that by the spring of 1911, the trend of business had become relatively stable, and awaited only appropriate incentives to revival. These incentives did not make their appearance until the close of 1911, and were in part the fruition of the sustaining influences which accompanied the readjustment process and mild depression. These influences were recognizable in the gradual recession of prices of manufactured articles until the latter part of 1911, with a violent upswing in prices of farm products and raw materials throughout the year, following their sharp decline in 1910; a fulfilling of contract orders during the greater part of 1910 and a consequent moderation of speculative enterprise; the working off upon domestic and foreign markets of overstocks acquired during the spirited industrial activity of 1909 and of the early part of 1910; a brisk export trade, insuring a fair volume of business at reasonably good prices; and a normal growth of consumption, paralleling increase in population. Because of this normal process of readjustment carried along on a basis of the sustaining influences above enumerated, the forces of depression were gradually converted into factors making for revival.[1]

Unmistakable signs of business revival became evident in the fall of 1911, just as they had in the fall of 1908. It is alleged by financial journals that business optimism was restored at this time because of favorable court decisions that laid down the " rule of reason " in the various trust cases.[2] This assertion is unjustified, in view of the fact that trust prosecutions thereafter continued in full swing. On the other hand, the causes of revival are to be discovered in certain favorable economic factors which were beginning to make their influence felt upon the industrial situation. Although agricultural production, except for cotton, was limited to moderate quantities, the prices of farm products soared throughout 1911. The cotton yield broke all records with nearly 16 million bales. Because of this huge return, which lowered the price of raw cotton, and because of past curtailment of output in the trade and the decreasing prices that had prevailed for cotton goods, the cotton drygoods trade improved considerably. Demand for materials and equipment by railroad had been light until the

[1] The following table gives fair indication of the decrease in purchasing power of the larger part of the consuming classes:

CROP YIELDS AND VALUE

(MILLION UNITS)

	Cotton		*Corn*		*Wheat*		*Rate of wages per week full time*	*Full time hours per week* *
	Bales	*Value*	*Bu.*	*Value*	*Bu.*	*Value*		
1909	10.3	$688	2,552	$1,653	683	$730	102	99
1910	11.9	820	2,886	1,385	635	561	104	99
1911	15.6	749	2,531	1,565	621	543	105	98

* Index No. of Bureau of Labor for 11 groups of industries—*Bulletin No. 194*.

[2] *Financial Review*, 1911, *Commercial and Financial Chronicle*, vol. xciii, pp. 5-15.

close of 1911, when large orders were placed.[1] The demand for copper from Europe, as well as from domestic sources, increased at the end of the year. The price of credit remained cheap and the application for investment funds proceeded on a moderate scale. After the revival got under way, the year of 1912 saw an uninterrupted business expansion from beginning to end. Such political factors as the presidential election, the Pujo Monetary Committee investigations, and the intensified trust prosecutions had no more restraining effect on the factors making for business expansion than did the unusually numerous labor disputes.

Improvements in the Security Market. The stock exchange was buoyant in the latter part of October, 1911, and continued so in November, with a recovery in prices and volume of sales; but, in December, it relapsed into a state of quiescence which lasted until March, 1912. During this latter period, considerable irregularity in prices was manifested, except for standard stocks, which were maintained. Prices of specialties receded. This lack of buoyancy was due largely to the decline in railroad earnings, the cut in prices of iron and steel,—tending toward lower profits for those concerns,—and the rather moderate yield of agricultural crops. The mild upswing in March, 1912, was well maintained in April. Starting from bed-rock prices, the bull movement was backed by powerful interests. "Rails" as well as "industrials" were buoyed up in price and in volume of sales. On the other hand, prices of bonds and their volume of turnover declined noticeably and steadily throughout the year. From April to August, prices of stocks made very little headway and total sales fell considerably. During August and the two following months, renewed activity occurred, but, although prices were forced

[1] *Railroad Age Gazette*, 1912.

up, the volume of security sales remained small. The public did not seem to be interested in the security market, and prices exhibited no strength, so that, when the movement receded, it left the level of prices considerably below that of 1906 and 1909. In November there began a downward revision of stock prices, striking bottom in June, 1913, on a level approximately halfway between that of December, 1907, and that of July, 1910.

PRICE TREND OF 12 INDUSTRIAL AND 40 RAILROAD STOCKS

	Industrials (Wall Street Jour.)			Railroad (Mitchell's Computation)		
	1911	1912	1913	1911	1912	1913
				L. H.	L. H.	L. H.
Feb.	85.2	80.9	81.2	250—267	230—241	211—227
July	85.9	89.9	77.2	255—265	235—245	192—205
Sept.	76.6	92.3 [a]	81.9	224—242	242—254 [a]	198—210
Dec.	80.9	88.0	77.1 [b]	240—252	228—242	185—199 [b]

[a] highest [b] lowest

This forcing down of the stock market, during the latter months of 1912, came about because of financial strain, and because of the rapid liquidation of American securities on foreign account, owing to war scares, abroad, which helped to undermine also the European security markets. It is estimated that thirty or forty million dollars worth of securities were thrown upon the New York stock exchange, by Europe, during the period from October 10 to 24.[1] To be sure, railroad earnings were large, crops were above normal, and industry and trade were very active, but these favorable conditions could not retard the collapse of the security market.

The European bourses exhibited a varying degree of strength during 1912. The first nine months witnessed a rise in security prices and an increasing volume of sales,

[1] *Cf. Chronicle*, vol. xcv, p. 1083.

stimulated by the vigorous industrial and trade development and the low price of credit which obtained during the first half of the year. This culminated in the latter part of the year, beginning with October, in an excessive speculation, leading to an abnormal state of affairs, and laying the basis for sharp reverses, because of political disturbances resulting from the Balkan crisis, and apprehensions of war. The decided activity in stock markets, generally, during the first nine months, together with the increase in production and trade, and the rise in prices, resulted in a closer interdependence between the money market and the bourses. This closer relationship was, however, impaired by factors resulting from the political complications that occurred. The pressure by governmental officials upon banks and the money market to meet political emergencies were indicated by: (1) the holding back of the British Treasury from the English money market; (2) the rapid liquidation of European banks generally; (3) the rigorous gold restrictions by the Bank of France; and (4) the cessation of Russian grain exports because of her inability to procure funds from the European banks. Credit extensions, owing to the strain in the investment market were limited largely to short-time loans which became subject to high rates in the fall of 1912. The shifting of funds among national markets, especially by the recalling of foreign loans, became a frequent practice. Money lenders became wary and cautious. Under these conditions a heavy liquidation set in during October and left the markets stunned for the remainder of the year.

The Paris bourse was under the stimulating influence of vigorous industrial activity, during the first three quarters of the year. In conjunction with the speculation in progress on the St. Petersburg bourse, there was a marked degree of overspeculation in domestic industrials and "Russians" during August and September. With the bourse in this condition, came the outbreak of the Balkan war. The result was such a heavy liquidation as to produce a panic in October, which was more severe than that which occurred at the outbreak of the Russian-Japanese war, in 1904. The heaviest losses were felt in Russian securities. By December, a mild recovery in security prices had set in, but it was not sufficient to overcome the momentum of the decline. The *Economiste Européen* reports a decrease, for the year, of 3.12 per cent in the value of 163 securities, this decline occurring principally during the panic days.

The German bourses began the year with a strong optimism, nurtured by cheap funds. Dampened somewhat in the beginning by strikes and political complications, this spirit of enterprise, with the industrial activity in progress, laid the basis for a vigorous upswing of security prices. Speculation was stimulated in particular by the exceptionally favorable conditons in the coal industry, as well as a like situation in the shipbuilding, iron and steel trades. Wholesome agricultural conditions also gave added impetus to the market. On October 1 and 2, with the outbreak of the Balkan war, a mild panic occurred on the Berlin bourse. This panic continued until October 14, when the Berlin banks took control of the situation, the saving feature being the fact that overspeculation had been restricted to a limited number of securities. During the latter part of the year the security market returned to normal conditions. The average price of all securities on the Berlin bourse assumed the following course:

	Interest-bearing	*Dividend-bearing*
1911 yearly average	94.34	162.45
1912—1st quarter	92.91	159.98
2nd quarter	92.05	158.85
3rd quarter	91.69	161.65
4th quarter	90.64	154.62
Yearly average	91.82	158.78

The London stock market reached its highest level in April, receding subsequently until July, when a recovery set in which continued until the latter part of September. During October, the excessive liquidation and decline of security prices on the continental bourses exerted a depressing influence. Dear money and the decline upon the New York stock market further forced down security prices. At the end of the year, British colonial railroad shares, especially the Canadian-Pacific, and several industrials, among which were the shipbuilding shares, were seen to have best maintained their ground, while the greatest price recession was to be observed in bonds and British railroad stocks, the latter being seriously affected by the coal strike. The average price of 387 securities declined 2.32 per cent.

Conditions in the Money Market. The money market in the United States, during 1912, remained in the state of extreme ease it had assumed in the previous year, until the month of July, when time-loan rates advanced and continued sharply upward until October, remaining at that level until December. The average advance in 60-90 day paper from July to October was from 4.53 per cent to 6 per cent. Rates for longer loans, also,—4 to 6 months,—increased correspondingly from 5.03 per cent to 6.50 per cent. Call-loan rates rose sharply from their easy position of 2.84 per cent in August to 6.50 per cent in December. The surplus reserves of New York banks diminished considerably, so that on November 28 there occurred a deficit of $5,198,000.

SURPLUS RESERVES OF NEW YORK BANKS (NOT INCLUDING TRUST COMPANIES)

(IN MILLION DOLLARS)

	1910	*1911*	*1912*
January 17	$30.3	$36.0	$41.3
March 21	14.2	31.0	7.6
May 16	23.8	45.6	19.1
July 11	27.1	5.7	8.0
September 12	23.4	22.6	3.0
November 28	11.8	2.4	5.1 (deficit)

The influences that affected the money market during the fall of 1912 may be summarized as follows: (1) the heavy demands from the interior for funds to move the abundant crops; (2) the recalling of gold and loans by Canadian banks; (3) extensive liquidation in the security markets in Europe, and the scramble for funds abroad, together with a general recalling of loans; (4) the high discount rates prevailing in Europe; (5) the need for funds for the general expansion of industry and trade together with the rising costs of materials and wages; and (6) the marked activity in grain speculation because of the possibility that war in the Balkans might cut off Russian grain exports. Exports of gold had taken place to a considerable extent during the first part of 1912, especially in January, February and May. Large quantities were sent directly to Paris in special transactions, and Paris also had some gold sent from here to South America. From August to December, however, imports of gold exceeded exports. This excess of imports was due principally to the outright purchases of South African gold on the London market, by New York bankers; to the abundance of cotton and grain bills; to the fairly high interest rates prevailing here; to the repurchasing, to some extent, of American securities by Europe; and to the imports of gold to this country, especially by Germany, in November. The effect of these favorable influences upon the money market, however, was delayed until January and February of 1913, when a sharp decline in interest rates took place.

Money rates eased off in all the European countries during the early part of the year. Official bank rates were marked down, so that by summer the London and Paris rates stood at the same level as in the previous year. The Berlin rate remained ½ per cent higher. Market rates at these three centers relaxed commensurately but continued higher than those in 1911. Seasonal tension developed on all markets, in September and October, as it did in the United States. The European money markets were subject to demand for funds, resulting from the upswing of industrial activity and high prices of materials, wages and foodstuffs, accompanied by speculation in commodities and securities. Large harvest yields together with the augmented purchasing power of the agricultural classes, and the heavy applications for capital made additional demands on funds. Other influences indirectly affecting the foreign money markets were to be found in the extensive preparations for war and the demand for goods resulting from wars in progress. Consequently, capital was in great demand. In addition the Balkan disturbances produced heavy liquidation of securities on European bourses in October. Simultaneously there developed a distrust in financial relationships between countries, which brought about a concentration of funds in domestic markets, except in England, where foreign interests, chiefly, were seeking and securing accommodations. The hoarding of specie became general.[1] During the scramble for gold from October to December the Reichsbank lost $46,000,000: the Bank of France, $27,000,000 gold and silver; and the Bank of England, $39,000,000. Because of the relative independence of the national markets the internal drains were the greater. Note issues increased in all countries. The Reichsbank possessed a substantially larger reserve of gold than that of the previous year. The increasingly favorable state of exchanges, on account of a growing export balance and the diminution of foreign withdrawals accomplished during the Moroccan crisis, enabled the Germany money market to meet the demands upon it, in spite of the fact that American

[1] *The Reichsbank Reports*, 1912, *passim.*

funds were withdrawn in the spring. This strong position of the money market aided the Berlin banks in actually taking a hand to arrest the security liquidation in October. The Bank of France, on the other hand, was face to face with the hoarding of specie. The unfavorable balance of trade had decreased because of better crops, and money became easier until fall, when the loss of specie by prevalent hoarding, forced higher rates. The situation in England was not very different; industrial prosperity was marked, and heavy demands for funds for foreign agricultural and investment purposes made themselves felt. The call upon London for gold from the interior as well as from the exterior was strong in the fall. Demands for gold from India, Egypt, and Germany from Brazil, Argentina and the United States were also heavy.

A.—GOLD MOVEMENTS ABROAD

(IN MILLION DOLLARS)

	Germany		*France*		*England*	
1911	*Exp.*	*Imp.*	*Exp.*	*Imp.*	*Exp.*	*Imp.*
First half	$4.8	$22.8	$15.0	$14.8	$75.6	$118.0
Second half	13.4	25.1	11.8	36.0	119.0	118.4
	$18.2	$47.9	$26.8	$50.8	$194.6	$236.4
1912						
First half	12.1	37.0	4.2	24.1	95.0	118.5
Second half	13.9	37.4	2.6	24.7	131.3	135.4
	$26.0	$74.4	$6.8	$48.8	$226.3	$253.4

B.—RESERVES AND CIRCULATION OF EUROPEAN BANKS

(IN MILLION DOLLARS)

	Reichsbank		*Bank of France*		*Bank of England*	
	Res.	*Cir.*	*Res.*	*Cir.*	*Res.*	*Cir.*
1910	$269	$417	$823	$1003	$132.4	$209
1911	288	431	779	1012	136.0	213
1912	295	460	778	1028	138.0	214

Production and Volume of Trade. The physical volume of production and business transactions assumed large proportions in all countries during 1912. In the United States, new records in production were established for many industries. Walter W. Stewart's index number of production shows the following relative increase:

Years	*All commodities*	*Total materials*	*Total manufactures*	*Total transportation*
1910	96	98	93	95
1911	93	93	92	92
1912	106	109	104	101

Bank clearings outside of New York show the growth in volume of business transactions. They were $66.8 billion in 1910; $67.6 in 1911; and $74.1 in 1912. Gross railroad earnings increased $47,900,000, the greatest increase being in the last half year. As in domestic trade, so also in foreign commerce there occured a marked expansion. Imports increased by $285 millions over 1911 and exports $341, making the favorable trade balance $55 million greater than in the previous year. Among the imports, foods and raw materials bulked largest, while among the exports, manufactured goods made the greatest increase.

Particular industries corroborate the growth in production, as shown by the index number above. Production of coal was 10 per cent greater than in 1911, an increase that occurred despite the largest suspension of labor ever experienced in that industry. In April and May of 1912, coal mining was almost completely halted in the anthracite field by the strike, which involved 500,000 miners, and the bituminous mines were running at only 35 per cent of their capacity. Nevertheless, the coal market was extremely favorable for the operators and a heavy production ensued. The suspension in April and May reduced the total anthracite production, but the bituminous fields showed a marked gain.

Copper production likewise increased, the total tonnage being 550,000 as against 489,800 in 1911. A great revival occurred in American consumption, and the European demand maintained itself during the first half of the year, though it diminished during the latter half. The overstocks accumulated during the depression were being reduced, and there was a considerable amount of future buying to be observed.

The iron and steel industry also responded to the general growth in production. The revisions in steel prices during the later months of 1911, to a point compatible with the general level of prices, laid a favorable price basis for steel products, upon which production could proceed. Pig-iron production responded likewise. The heavy production in 1910 in this industry left a large stock to be worked off during 1911.[1] These stocks were completely absorbed in 1912 and there was a further production of 29,727,000 gross tons—a record volume, 2½ millions more, in fact than in 1910, and 6 mllions more than in 1911. Capacity output was continued throughout the year and contracts carried it well into 1913. The unfilled orders of the U. S. Steel Corporation grew in volume until the very last month of 1912, the increase being from 5,380,000 tons per month in January to 7,932,000 in December. Railroad orders were quite extensive. Freight car orders, for example, numbered 226,195 in 1912 as against 183,117 in 1911. Cars actually built in these years totalled 148,357 and 70,931 respectively.

Government reports of crop conditions during 1912 estimated cotton and wheat as progressively unfavorable, and corn as favorable. The final harvests yielded unprecedented quantities of corn, wheat, and oats, while cotton production, except for a shortage in India, was also very large,

[1] *Statistical Bulletin*, Am. Iron and Steel Institute, no. 6, 1913.

though it did not quite attain the huge total of the previous year. The corn yields of Argentina and Austria-Hungary were especially large, as was the wheat yield in France, Germany and Russia. These abundant crops exerted a powerful influence upon business generally in spite of the fact that prices of farm products, after attaining a remarkably high level, began to decline in May.

Production statistics indicate a marked expansion of industry and trade abroad. In Germany the coal and metal industries, as well as manufacturing, flourished. The tightness of the money market reacted somewhat unfavorably upon building, which in turn, affected the paint, glass, wood, and related industries; but otherwise, the year 1912 was one of cumulative prosperity. Germany's foreign trade increased proportionally more than that of the United States, France and England, though the unfavorable trade balance increased. Among the import items, food, raw materials and raw textiles showed the greatest increase. Manufactured articles and minerals were the largest factors in exports. Indexes of domestic industry and trade, such as bills of exchange in circulation, earnings of railroads, and bank clearings evidenced a great expansion in France and disclosed a marked recovery from the relaxation of business activity that was characteristic of the greater part of 1911, owing to the crop failure of 1910. France's foreign commerce increased, thereby reducing the unfavorable trade balance, which amounted to $100,000,000, to a figure below that of 1911. There was a great decrease in the importation of food and an increase in its exportation. The greatest increase in exports was in manufactured products.

If we consult the indexes of the general volume of business, we discover a continuous growth and expansion in England in 1912. Considerable labor trouble, however, caused a contraction in coal, iron, and steel production. In

March 2,000,000 coal miners walked out and in July the dockworkers struck. Unemployment, outside of strikes, was maintained at a very low percentage during the year. Good harvests generally and a world-wide prosperity including the strong revival in the United States brought very favorable conditions for England's broad markets. Thus her foreign trade expanded to the extent of $267 millions imports and $160 millions in exports. The unfavorable trade balance increased, however, from $601 to $708. Imports gained $97 millions for wholly or partly manufactured goods, $131 for raw materials, and $83 for foods. Exports gained $112 millions, $29, and $15 respectively for these three classes of commodities.[1]

PRODUCTION AND TRADE INDEXES OF THE UNITED KINGDOM

	1910		*1911*		*1912*	
Coal production (million long tons)	264		272		260	
Pig iron production (million long tons)	10.0		9.5		8.7	
Railroad earnings, gross (million dollars)	556		570		576	
London bank clearings (million dollars)	713		711		777	
Imports (million dollars)	2,796		2,812		3,079	
Exports (million dollars)	2,094	(—702)	2,211	(—601)	2,371	(—708)

[1] It is to be noted that England experienced considerable competition in both home and foreign markets during these years. The unusual number of labor difficulties further impaired their condition. The metal industries met with considerable rivalry from those of Germany and the United States. U. S. Steel Corporation exports increased as follows:

Year	*Gross tons*
1908	775,345
1909	985,474
1910	1,195,465
1911	1,708,487
1912	2,243,138

England's overproduction in 1911 seems to have been the result of the expansion of that industry in Germany, and the increased exports of steel by the United States, which created a lack of markets for English steel products. Up to 1911 the rate of increase in production of iron and steel in the United Kingdom followed a perfectly normal course, while

Diverse Movements of Commodity Prices. The price movements of commodities during this period, indicate their usual relative trends. The U. S. Bureau of Labor Index of general wholesale commodity prices shows a sharp advance, from 129.2 in December, 1911, to 135.4 in May, 1912, an advance which held for the balance of the year. Manufactured commodities as shown by the same statistics, rose in price with raw materials and farm products, until April and May, when farm products and raw materials declined sharply, while prices of manufactured articles continued to advance, and reached their zenith at the close of the year.

WHOLESALE PRICES IN THE UNITED STATES IN 1912

	All commodities	*Manufactured articles*	*Farm products*	*Raw materials*
Jan.	130.5	126.1 [b]	171.6	148.3
Apr.	134.8	128.7	189.0	160.1 [a]
May	135.4 [a]	129.9	189.8 [a]	157.8
Sept.	135.2	131.6	166.3	147.4
Dec.	135.1 [b]	132.8 [a]	157.8 [b]	144.9 [b]

[a] *highest* [b] *lowest*

Prices of raw materials began their sharp decline after April and, notwithstanding a slight effort toward recovery in the fall, continued lower until the close of 1912. Prices of farm products soared to unprecedented levels until April and May, followed by a sharp decline which continued until January, 1913. We find in this development, movements

subsequently a decline set in. A perusal of the export statistics of manufactured products of England lead to similar conclusions:

INCREASE OF EXPORTS

Year	*Increase in million $'s*
1909	0
1910	224
1911	97
1912	112

of prices similar to that in 1907, but, unlike the retrogression of prices in 1910, when prices of all commodities moved downward together, varying only in degree. Retail prices, after their phenomenal rise in the last half of the preceding year, experienced a check in the early part of 1912, as a result of generally good harvests. This halt, however, was temporary, and they subsequently continued to advance throughout 1912. This tendency toward increasing cost of living was a predominant characteristic of this period in most countries.

Prices of some of the basic products such as steel, pig iron and copper, indicate a decided advance during the whole year. Steel products began to rise in April, and reached approximately the level of prices attained in the early part of 1910. Pig-iron prices reacted sympathetically, though they did not participate in the advance until August, when the overstocks began to be worked off. This rise was checked in November, when about 12 per cent of its 20 per cent decline from the 1909 level had been regained. Copper prices advanced more noticeably than they did in 1906. The average price per pound in 1912 varied from 14 cents in January to 17.3 cents in November. This advance was made possible by the increased consumption of copper in Europe and a decrease in surplus stocks here.

In general, prices of commodities in Europe advanced throughout the year. In Germany, the index number of wholesale prices, computed from the data published in the *Vierteljahrshefte zur Statistik des Deutschen Reichs,* increased from 128 in 1911 to 140 in 1912. Sauerbeck's index number for England varied from 123 to 130, while that of the *Annuaire Statistique* for France increased from 126 to 131. During the last quarter of the year, however, the trend of prices generally pursued a halting course.

Demand for Investment Funds at Home and Abroad. The investment market in the United States, during 1912, reflected a strong demand for industrial capital in the large volume of security issued. New issues of railroad securities, stocks, and bonds, however, were very small, listings on the New York stock exchange having reached a lower level than in 1907, for the reason that the increased earnings of railroad companies reduced borrowing. Public utilities, on the other hand, showed heavy issues. The total issue of stocks was made up largely of industrials, and proved to be the largest of any year since 1907. Bond issues were large, in spite of the congestion in the domestic and foreign bond markets and the higher interest rates prevailing during the latter half of 1912. Promotions continued actively, in spite of the alleged discouragement due to extensive investigations of trusts and combinations, such as that conducted by the Pujo Monetary Committee, which carried on a wide and sweeping inquiry into money and credit conditions, or the suits under the Sherman Act, brought against a large number of combinations carrying on business in a variety of products.[1] The resulting tendency toward voluntary offers to dissolve combinations upon governmental advice was neutralized somewhat by acquittals in important trust cases, and promotion proceeded as usual.

Those additions to industrial equipment which had re-

[1] Suits brought against the Coffee Valorization plan implicating the Brazilian Government. Harvester Company—Powder Trust (May); Aluminum Trust (May); Pacific Coast Plumbing Supply Association (Aug.); Central West Publishing Co. (Aug.); National Packing Co. (June) voluntary; National Cash Register Co. (Feb.); American-Asiatic Steamship Co. (June); Prince Line (Dec.); Kellog Toasted Corn Flakes Co. Indictment of C. S. Mellen of N. H. & N. H. R. R.; Chicago Beef Packers acquitted (Mar.); Bath Trust Case (Nov.) patent rights decision; Terminal R. R. Association of St. Louis (Apr.); U. P. & So. P. merger illegal (Dec.); Anthracite Coal Combine illegal (Dec.).

sulted from the remarkable promotions of business enterprises, during the boom period preceding the panic of 1907, and also from the heavy capital expenditures during the following period up to 1912, had not been completely utilized. The relatively quiescent spirit in investment enterprise that developed during the latter part of 1912 in comparison with 1906 and 1909 is explained by the adequate capacity of the existing industrial equipment, and the restraints imposed upon further use of investment funds by the stresses that were engendered in the investment market at that time. But the need for working capital was strong, and heavy security issues to meet this need were floated; also, many new security issues were the result of the prevalent business reorganizations. The listings of new stock issues upon the New York stock exchange was $464 millions in 1921 as against $256 millions in 1911, while that of bonds increased from $397 millions to $448 millions in 1912. Building operations, if judged by the value of permits issued, according to the reports of 20 selected cities as well as those of 206 cities, give evidence of no great increase in activity of construction work during 1912. This fact seems to indicate that business enterprise sought funds by security issues for working capital and reorganizations rather than for expansion of building operations or of industrial equipment.

New applications for capital in Germany, France and England were greater than they were in 1911, but relaxed during the later months. The complexion of the continental demand points to a decided isolation of the various capital markets, a great advance in domestic industrial stocks, and a decline of foreign issues, while all European countries were characterized by a much greater increase in stock emissions as compared with those of bonds. Bond issues were retarded because of the higher interest rates that developed. In England, however, there was evidence of a many-sided domestic and foreign capital need. Railroad issues of the colonies and of North and South America were large, Russian railroads too voiced heavy requirements. Rubber and oil shares were emitted in large volumes. Domestic issues increased, especially in industrials. Upon the continent, particularly in Germany, government loans were put forth again in large amounts, though in France they remained lower than those of 1911; and in both countries domestic government loans increased greatly.

SECURITY ISSUES IN GERMANY, FRANCE AND ENGLAND
(IN MILLION DOLLARS)

				Private	
France	*Total*	*Foreign Gov'ts.*	*Domestic Gov'ts.*	*Stocks*	*Bonds*
1910	$1,122	$340	$21	$447	$314
1911	922	195	1.5	324	401
1912	1,048	145	61	558	284
Germany				*(Dividenden-Papiere)*	*(Festverzinsliche-Werte)*
1910	644	53	204	126	261
1911	570	68	130	124	248
1912	607	18	238	143	202
England				*Miscellaneous* *	*Industrial*
1910	1,301	90	128	538 *	545
1911	923	118	12	423 *	380
1912	1,026	46	1.4	454 *	525

* — percentage of foreign issues were 20.6%, 20.5% and 23.0% for 1910—11-12 respectively.

Attempts to obtain new capital were greatly restricted during the latter part of 1912, because the universal monetary stringency that developed interfered with the absorption of the huge emissions previously made. In addition, war preparations and industrial requirements made themselves felt in a simultaneous demand upon the capital market. The increase in supply of capital, furthermore, was retarded by the effect upon savings of the rising cost of living. The result was a capital famine.

Use of Loan Credit. Measured by the expansion of loans and discounts of national banks and the New York clearing-house banks, use of bank credit in the United States during 1912 increased more than in 1909, in spite of slight retardation in loan expansion in the fall, due to the high interest rates, developed during the liquidation of the security market, looking to the approaching exhaustion of bank reserves.

	All National Banks		New York Clearing House Banks		
	(in million dollars)				
1912	*Loans, etc.*	*Individual Deposits*	*Average for*	*Loans, etc.*	*Net Deposits*
Feb. 20	$5,834	$5,632	Feb.	$1,422	$1,482
Apr. 18	5.902	5,713	Apr.	1,389	1,410
June 14	5.974	5,827	June	1,398	1.453
Sept. 4	6,061	5,893	Sept.	1,357	1.359
Nov. 26	6,085	5.946	Nov.	1,310	1,292

The statement of the Joint Stock Banks of England also indicate an expansion of loans, but a halting increase toward the close of 1912:

	(in million dollars)	
	Loans, etc.	*Deposits and current accounts*
1911—May	$2,277	$3.507
Nov.	2,318 (+41)	3.571 (+65)
1912—May	2,362 (+44)	3.643 (+72)
Nov.	2,391 (+29)	3,661 (+18)

On the continent, the policy of credit extension assumed a complicated aspect. The statements of the German Joint Stock Banks indicate the unusual banking conditions following 1910, conditions which also held good to a great extent of France. These seem to have been the result mainly of the political influences that were there at work and of various other factors that produced disturbances upon the money and investment markets. From a study of the reports of the German Joint Stock Banks, we may draw the following conclusions as to the changes in the chief items in the statements, from the previous year. The plus and minus quantities indicate thousand dollars:

	1910	*1911*	*1912*
Discounts	+ 45,905	— 4,851	— 3,061
Advances and contangoes	+ 42,557	+ 7,805	—23,568
Underwriting operations	+ 7,567	— 3,932	+ 18,288
Bills receivable	+ 152,691	+ 83,368	+ 20,312
Closed deposits	+ 61,692	+ 57,176	+ 32,785
Deposits on current acct.	+ 127,147	— 17,670	— 51,088

The contraction of bank credit seems to have begun in 1911 with considerable decrease in deposits on current account and no great increase in time deposits. Universal caution in credit granting became very apparent by the year 1912. The conservative credit policies of European banks seems to have been responsible largely for the heavy issues of securities during the year.

According to bank reports, loans and discounts, as well as the note circulation of the Reichsbank and of the Bank of France, increased during the whole year, and especially in the latter months. The increase in these items seems to indicate exhaustion in the lending power of private banks and a falling back upon the great central banks.

Business Profits. Profits in industry were generally very good, as indicated by profit data. Nevertheless, there was a striking increase in the number of commercial failures, as compared with the total number of firms in business. After the panic of 1907, the number of these failures decreased until 1910, when they again began to mount, continuing to do so throughout 1911 and 1912. The increasing cost of doing business was due chiefly to labor unrest, dearness of materials, difficulties in the financial markets, and the close competition growing out of the huge combines that came into existence just before and immediately following 1907. These industrial combinations, which had by this time orientated themselves relative to their economic and legal milieu, worked fatal results to the smaller independent concerns.

Political Factors. Though 1912 was a presidential year, with a Democratic victory almost assured, no disturbance in industrial and trade conditions was noticeable. Reforms in our banking system were in the air; this prospect might be construed as the only political factor favorable to business. Tariff revision downward became a certainty. Trust prosecutions continued and additional anti-trust legislation by the new party was assured, although the meaning and intent of these was somewhat clarified by the courts. Labor troubles were numerous and strikes were prevalent at home and abroad. The fear that all the large powers would become involved in the Balkan controversy produced considerable disturbance in Europe. Although this led at the close of 1912 to an unprecedented scramble for funds everywhere and to a drain upon the investment and money markets, production and trade still continued to make progress.

CHAPTER VI

The Depression of 1913

The Early Termination of Prosperity. The brief prosperity of 1912 was followed in the United States by an immediate reaction in 1913. Although the universal cycle, also, came to what seemed to be a premature completion in Germany, France and England, the business recession in this country began fully six months earlier than it did abroad.[1] There, the tempo of business was only slightly retarded and the reaction set in only during the closing months of the year,—liquidation in the security markets beginning in the second half of the year and commodity markets remaining almost untouched. In the United States, however, signs of a business reaction began at the very opening of the year. The liquidation in the security market, which had begun in the fall of 1912, was complete by June of 1913. Prices of raw materials had begun to fall in the early part of 1912, but prices of finished products declined slowly, holding up remarkably in 1913. For a good part of the year, the physical volume of business remained large because of the heavy orders originating in the boom of 1912 and because of a large agricultural production, but after old contracts had been filled no current demand developed to bolster up business activity, and the latter part of the year saw a decided recession.

Normality of the Liquidation Process. The year 1913 was characterized by a gradual decline in business activity

[1] *Cf. Com. and Fin. Chronicle*, vol. xcviii, pp. 5-16; *cf. Volkswirtschaftliche Chronik*, 1913, pp. 901 *et seq.*; *cf. London Economist*, vol. lxxviii, pp. 3-4.

and a normal liquidation process, which passed slowly into a state of acute depression. The depression took hold of the United States during the last months of 1913, and of England, France, and Germany during the spring of 1914. This absence of sudden and violent disruption of business relationships, as the result of a highly accelerated liquidation process, is common to European transitional periods, but is rather unique in the recent annals of American business with the one exception, possibly, of 1910. Prosperity, with us, has been wont to recede with a sudden collapse of prices and production. But the year 1912 saw no excessive capitalization, following as it did upon the heels of the reaction of 1910-11, and the incentives seem to have been inadequate for any such overreaching by the spirit of enterprise as had occurred in previous boom periods,—for example, that which preceded the panic of 1907.

Decline of the Security Market. The New York stock exchange began to show signs of weakening in November and December of 1912. It must be observed that the security market had evinced no striking activity since its collapse in 1910, following the phenomenal progress made during the boom of 1908-09, when it attained a general price level comparable to that of 1904-05. The recovery in prices of securities in 1911 and 1912 was only moderate and the volume of sales was of even less significance relative to the rise in prices. Moreover, the rise in securities during the mild return of activity on the stock market in 1911-12 was limited to the industrial stocks, while bonds generally had continued to decline since the beginning of 1909, and railroad stocks followed a similar course from the opening of 1910. The interruption of 1910-11 in the downward course of bonds, and that of 1912 in the falling value of railroad stocks, were of little significance. The security market struck bottom in June, 1913, and remained in a state of inertia until after the outbreak of the world war. Not since the year 1897 had the volume of security sales been so low as they were in 1913.

This decline in security values was the result, partly of the high interest rates developed, during the financial strain that existed with only a temporary relaxation from the close of 1912 until the end of 1913, especially in the long-time funds. Heavy liquidation of securities on foreign account, the diminishing rate of industrial activity, and the rather heavy issues of new securities also played their part, as did the decline in railroad earnings, caused by the policy of the Interstate Commerce Commission in refusing applications for advances in rates. The demoralization of the stock market was augmented to a considerable extent by conditions prevailing in the European bourses, which, toward the middle of the year, became disorganized, and subject to active and persistent liquidation. Relative prices of stocks and bonds and the volume of stock and bond sales on the New York Stock Exchange are given below:

	Monthly Average of			*Volume of sales*	
	10 railroad bonds[c]	*12 industrial stocks (Wall Street Journal)*	*40 railroad bonds*[c] (*Low*) — (*High*)	*bonds (par value in million dollars)*	*stocks (million shares)*
1912					
Jan.	108.0	81.3	230 — 244	$111[a]	11
June	106.7	89.7	237 — 247	44	7
Oct.	105.0	92.3[a]	238[a] — 253[a]	45	14[a]
Dec.	104.8	88.0	228 — 242	43	13
			Year's total		131
1913					
Jan.	105.4	85.1	222 — 235	53	9
June	99.2	74.7[b]	186[b] — 204[b]	39[b]	10
Oct.	99.8	79.3	192 — 204	39	7
Dec.	98.1	77.1	185 — 199	47	7
			Year's total		84

[a] *highest* [b] *lowest*

[c] Computations based on W. C. Mitchell's selection previously referred to.

There was a diminishing activity during 1913 on the German bourses, characterized by a halting rise in stock prices during the first half-year, and a decline during the second. Bond prices receded throughout the year, even those of standard bonds reaching record-breaking low levels. The German 3 per cent Imperials, for example, fell off from 83.6 in 1911, to 75.9 in 1913. This restriction in the prices and the volume of sales of securities was due to the political disturbances arising from the Balkan war, which, together with the strong industrial activity, produced a stringency in the investment market. Because of shaken confidence, the public, generally, remained uninterested in security trading, and speculation was dampened. The scramble for gold, hoarding, and the general contraction of credit by all large financial institutions played havoc on the bourses. The decline in prices affected principally the mining, machine industry and the terrain-association shares. Shipping shares remained very active until effected by a rate war among the shipping interests. The course of average prices in all interest-bearing and dividend-yielding securities on the Berlin bourse, and of the volume of sales, indicated by the tax yield, are as follows:

	Interest-bearing	*Dividend-yielding*	*Bourse Sales Tax Yield (thousand dollars)*
Yearly average—1912...	91.82	158.78	Total for 1912—$6,207
Dec. 1912..................	90.78	154.89	323
1st quarter—1913	90.48	158.58	335
2nd quarter—1913.	89.18	157.31	440
3rd quarter—1913.........	88.68	158.09	332
4th quarter—1913.........	88.81	156.39	303
Yearly average—1913...	89.31	157.59	Total for 1913— 4,230

The Paris bourse, also, evidenced a small volume of sales, and a low ebb in prices. The *Economiste Européen* reports a decrease in the average price of 163 securities of 2.70 per cent in 1913, as against a decline of 3.60 per cent during the previous year. The greatest depreciation occurred in the Rentes, closely followed by industrial stocks. The almost complete stagnation of business upon the bourse, in view of high interest rates, caused a severe fall in the prices of fixed-interest-bearing securities, which was not offset even by the comparative firmness of railroad and bank stocks. It must be observed that the bourse had labored in a state of depression since 1912, when its chief trading items had become undermined by war, revolution and decline in the prices of coffee and rubber. Because of the fear of war, the rising cost of living, and the attack on wealth by Premier Caillaux, especially with reference to taxation, foreign investments were freely sought, and most transactions were carried on through banks outside of the speculative area and the bourse.[1]

Monetary stringency, and restraint on the part of the investors, influenced the London stock exchange throughout the year. All security values declined. There was an almost complete absence of speculation, and the public was bearish.[2] The Balkan wars and the Mexican revolution, together with the heavy issues of new securities, exerted a marked influence in the market. Foreign securities depreciated considerably, especially American railroads, and the Mexican and Brazilian shares. Rubber and mining shares showed the greatest decline, prices of rubber shares falling 49.3 per cent. The protracted crumbling of raw rubber prices as well as of coffee undermined the values of Brazilian shares. In addition to this, there was the minor

[1] *Cf.* B. M. Anderson, Jr., *Effects of the War on Money, Credit and Banking in France and the United States*, pp. 36 *et seq.*

[2] *Cf. London Economist*, vol. xcviii, p. 4, quoted: "It is easy, of course, to say that any year—especially one which has just finished—has been the worse on record, but a combination of events rendered 1913 a specially lean period, for even where jobbing firms, for example, have been sufficiently lucky to make money on their dealing, the depreciation of securities on their books has been literally enormous."

financial crisis in China. In spite of prevalent labor troubles at home, domestic securities stood their ground better than foreign securities. Banking, insurance and brewery companies' issues remained firm. The contraction of loans in all the great European money markets exerted a depressing influence on the stock exchanges. The decline of the total value of 387 securities on the London stock exchange, as computed by the *London Bankers' Magazine*, was 5.3 per cent, the greatest decline in many years.

Tendencies in the Money Market. The money market in New York opened with a state of absolute ease during January, 1913. The heavy exportation of gold that had taken place was offset to a considerable degree by the return of funds from the interior. Large gold exports continued, however, caused by the heavy selling of railroad securities by Europeans in the New York market and the eagerness of France to obtain gold either directly or on Argentine account. Consequently, interest rates on time-money rose until August, with only a slight temporary relaxation in April and May, 1913. Rates on call-money, on the other hand, except for a slight upward reaction in March, as a result of the gold outflow, continued low until the latter part of the year, when they reacted to the general demand for funds. This lower rate on call-money was brought about partly by the refusal of the National City Bank to observe the 3 per cent minimum rate. Time-loan rates became easier from September to December, and in January, 1914, rates on all money sank to extremely low levels. The interior demand for funds was met, to a large extent, by the decision of the Secretary of the treasury to deposit Government money with banks in the West and South for purposes of crop movement. Gold imports from England, also, aided in alleviating the strain in the fall. The movement of money rates in the New York market was as follows:

1912	Call loans	60–90 day paper	4–6 months paper
Nov.	6.38%	5.75%	6.50%
1913			
Jan.	3.35	4.61	5.21
Mar.	4.19	5.75	6.25
May	2.75	5.34	5.88
Aug.	2.28	6.00	6.63
Dec.	4.13	5.72	6.34
1914			
Feb.	1.78	3.84	4.38

Gold exportations were moderately heavy during the first four or five months of the year and met only a temporary check in August, September and October. The total exports for 1913 was $91,790,000, as against $63,705,000, in imports. France remained a persistent bidder for the metal, often paying a premium, while considerable shipments were also made to Germany, Venezuela, and Canada, Special transactions in gold were frequent, executed largely by Paris.

The reserve position of the New York clearing-house banks was slightly better in 1913, than it was in 1912. The percentage of gain was as follows:

	1912	*1913*
1st quarter	26.75%	25.86%
2nd quarter	26.28	26.80
3rd quarter	25.77	26.39
4th quarter	25.36	25.69

However, the absolute amount of surplus reserves of New York banks, not including trust companies, was notably low in the early part of 1913, and again, during the fall months. The decided contraction of deposits and loans, which began to show in the statements of the New York clearing-house banks in the fall of 1912, continued during 1913. Bankers' balances as well as individual deposits declined in the banks of the reserve cities. The reserve position of the banks had been, for some time, subject to heavy gold withdrawals for export and, therefore, no great recovery in their reserve position occurred in 1913, in spite of the depression. The ratio of reserves to deposits, also, was lower in 1913, than in 1912, for all national banks. The banking situation thus indicates the strong demand for funds that existed in this country during the year.

European Money Market. The money market abroad felt the influence both of industrial activity and of political anxiety. Stringency prevailed, and unusually heavy demands were made upon the banks until past the middle of the year. The relaxation in demand, which took place from July onward, was the result of moderation in the great pressure in important business branches as well as of a diminution of activity on the bourses, and the gradual return of money hoarded during the preceding year. Political complications appeared less imminent in the latter part of 1913 and there was a general restoration of confidence. All countries, moreover, were stocking up with gold,—another factor that helped to lower money rates at the close of the year. Some of the features of the European monetary conditions are set forth below:

A. Estimated Amounts Hoarded in Europe in 1912 [1]

French people	$150 millions
German people	130 millions

B. European Gold Movement in Million Dollars

	Germany		*France*		*England*	
	Imp.	*Exp.*	*Imp.*	*Exp.*	*Imp.*	*Exp.*
…2	$74.4	$26.0	$43.8	$6.8	$253.9	$226.3
…3	73.1	14.8	127.9	14.5	296.7	208.0
…4	22.3	7.7 (6 mos.)	55.0	9.0 (5 mos.)	122.5	126.7 (6 mo
	169.8	48.5	226.7	30.3	673.1	561.0

[1] *Cf. Chronicle*, vol. xcvii, pp. 1851 *et seq.*

C. Amount of Gold Reserves of European Central Banks

(millions of dollars)

	Reichsbank	*Bank of France*	*Bank of Engla[nd]*
1912	$295	$772 (gold and silver)	138
1913	329	761	133
1914 (7 months)	403	838	141

All banks in 1913 were seeking to strengthen their reserves, and these efforts made themselves felt in the gold market.[1] In this attempt, Europe was greatly aided by the release of gold from North and South America. In the United States, this release was made possible by the business reaction in the early months of 1913, when gold was employed to a great extent in paying interest and capital debts in Europe, particularly in France. Brazil and Argentina, also, returned a quantity of gold which had been withdrawn from Europe in previous years, largely for the reason that the export of capital to these countries was now restricted and other loans were partly liquidated. Brazil's unfavorable trade situation, especially, owing to the decline in her chief exports,—coffee and rubber,—made shipment of gold to Europe unavoidable. India, also, asked for less gold in 1913, but sought to strengthen its credits in Europe. When war had ceased in the Balkans, money eased, somewhat, and the weakening of industrial activity in the fall produced a further relaxation of money rates during the last quarter of the year.

Interest rates abroad were higher than they were in 1912, although, in Germany, there was a supply of funds sufficient to avoid any undue financial strain. Moreover, the increasingly favorable trade balance of that country operated to the added advantage of the credit market. However, the demands for capital and credit continued quite persistently. The formation of banking kartells, (Kondition-

[1] *Ibid.*, vol. xcvi, p. 310.

enkartell) for the purpose of controlling the liquidation process and restraining undue speculation, seriously impaired the free operation of economic factors in the credit market. This extraordinary effort of the banks to ensure a normal liquidation process was the most outstanding feature of the German money market in 1913.

France felt a persistence of internal demands for funds, for hoarding still prevailed to some degree, and industry was active during the first part of the year; there was, in addition, a heavy flow of capital into economically backward and foreign countries. The political controversy in progress over a progressive income tax, and the increasingly unfavorable trade balance produced further stringency. These factors shook the position of France as a world banker. France was also required to make financing possible for the Balkans, in order that the security prices of those countries in which the French had invested heavily might be maintained after the Balkan peace.

The money market in England was affected by several factors; internal labor difficulties, "Home Rule", increased taxes, and the extension of naval and social programs. International influences were equally disturbing. Although the Balkan situation exerted no direct influence, continental demands for gold, as an indirect result, drew heavily upon the English gold market. In addition, demands for capital from the colonies, and from Brazil, Argentina, China, and Mexico, remained persistent. The first two countries named were experiencing especially trying financial difficulties. The failure of the India Specie Bank added a further complication. It is a significant fact that the great financial institutions were congested by unabsorbed securities, and that underwriting operations required a great quantity of funds.

The course of official and private discount rates, in the

European money markets, is indicative of the financial strain that existed until the close of the year, and the return of universal low interest rates at the beginning of 1914:

	Germany		France		England	
1912	*Bank*	*Private*	*Bank*	*Private*	*Bank*	*Private*
Dec.	6.00%	5.94%	4.00%	3.90%	5.00%	4.84%
1913						
Feb.	6.00	5.15	4.00	3.93	5.00	4.78
Apr.	5.00	5.90	4.00	4.00	4.70	3.89
Aug.	6.00	4.88	4.00	3.75	4.50	3.78
Nov.	5.50	4.45	4.00	3.73	5.00	4.90
1914						
Feb.	4.25	3.11	4.00	2.92	3.00	2.96

Movement of Commodity Prices. The movement of prices in 1913 was curious. The index number of the Bureau of Labor, for general wholesale prices, indicates that the sharp rise in the earlier months of 1912 culminated in May of that year, and that, thereafter, prices continued on that high level until the slight rise in September and October. Subsequently, prices declined and continued to do so in 1914. A closer examination of prices in the separate classes of commodities indicates that farm products rose throughout 1913 except for a temporary recession in the summer months. Prices of raw materials on the other hand declined until July, when they, also, rose sharply. These two groups of commodities had witnessed a short and sharp decline in prices in May 1912. One of the striking features of the period from 1907 to 1914 is the marked advance in the secular price trend of farm products and raw materials. Manufactured articles, on the other hand, showed a gradual recession, throughout 1913, the total being moderate. Relative wholesale prices of commodities in the United States during the period under consideration are given below, computed by the Bureau of Labor.

1912	*All commodities*	*Farm products*	*Raw materials*	*Manufactured products*
May	135.4	*189.8*[b]	*157.8*[b]	129.9
Dec.............	135.1	*157.8*[a]	*144.9*[a]	132.8[b]
1913				
Mar.............	135.1	166.3	145.4	132.6
July	*134.3*[a]	162.7	*144.2*[a]	131.9
Dec..............	*135.7*[b]	171.8	154.4	*131.2*[a]

[a] *lowest* [b] *highest*

Retail prices, as indicated by the Bureau of Labor Statistics, made striking advances in 1913, especially after the first five months, rising from 98.1 in January to 103.9 in December.

Some of the important particular commodity markets recorded a decrease in prices. Those of steel products and pig iron began to slide in April and, by the end of 1913, reached the low level of 1911. Prices of copper receded, on an average, about one cent per lb. for the year. Prices of raw cotton, on the other hand, rose above those of 1912, and made sharp advances during the last months of 1913, because of a small harvest yield.

In Germany, France, and England; prices continued to rise during the first quarter of 1913, culminating in the second quarter, when a recession began, which characterized the rest of the year. In this decline, prices of foods figured most prominently. The relative trend of wholesale prices in Germany, France, and England was as follows:

	Germany Vierteljahrshefte zur Statistik	*France Statistique Generale*	*England*	
			Sauerbeck	*Economist*
1912—average......	140	117.8	115.9	123.4
1913—average.....	139	115.6	115.9	122.3
1913—1st quarter..	*	116.2	117.6	123.6
1913—2nd quarter	*	116.7	116.2	122.6
1913—3rd quarter	*	115.1	115.7	122.5
1913—4th quarter	*	114.3	114.1	120.7

* no price data available

Trend in Volume of Production and Trade. The volume of production in the United States began to decline at the beginning of 1913, while trade continued in considerable volume. Bank clearings outside of New York City diminished in volume, but moderately,[1] the decrease being mild in comparison with that of 1907 and 1910. Gross earnings of railroads declined in proportion to the decrease in 1910. The contraction in the volume of domestic trade was gradual and did not become great until the latter months of 1913. Foreign commerce underwent a retardation in its growth, but was greater than that of 1912. Imports declined during the first half, but in the last half of the year they made substantial gains. Exports decreased more during the last half of the year than in the first half. The excess of merchandise exports over imports increased to the extent of $1·10 millions in 1913. Importations of raw materials and manufactured articles increased greatly, while those of foodstuffs declined. Manufactured articles and foodstuffs gained in exports, while raw materials remained static. The above conclusions are borne out by W. W. Stewart's index number of general production. All commodities declined from 106, in 1912, to 101 in 1913. Total materials decreased from 109 to 98, total manufactures remained at 104, while total transportation gained from 101 to 106. These figures show that trade maintained an ample volume and that the decline was largely in the production of materials.

If statistics of production in the particular industries are examined, it is found that their trends varied. Coal production ran high for the year, but diminished at the close.[2] Pig-iron production was exceedingly high for most of the year, but contracted suddenly in November. Steel produc-

[1] This is to be largely explained by the sustained price level.

[2] *Mineral Industry*, vol. xxii, p. 88.

tion fared similarly.[1] The huge unfilled orders, accumulated in the preceding year, were of considerable aid to this industry, as were the active war preparations going on in Europe. During 1913, the U. S. Steel Corporation felt a severe contraction in unfinished orders—a drop, in fact, from 7,827,000 tons, in January, to 4,282,000 in December. The other important metal, copper, also showed a moderate contraction in production.[2] Monthly statistics indicate that, although in some of these industries production was diminished, as a whole, a good volume was maintained during the greater part of the year, which receded, noticeably, only during the last few months of 1913. Manufacturing continued fairly strong during the first half-year, but decreased in the second, evidently, because of the fact that prices for these products continued fairly high. War preparations in Europe exerted a noticeable influence on the metal industries generally. The agricultural yield in the United States was materially reduced by heat and drought. Although wheat and oats were above normal, and cotton yielded more than an average crop, these did not offset the poor corn yield which was 700 million bushels under that of 1912. A study of crop statistics, in detail, indicates, moreover that the per acreage yield was not as favorable as the total yield would lead one to believe. In other parts of the world, agricultural returns were very good. Indian cotton and Russian and Canadian wheat yielded noticeably large crops. Many countries showed returns above the normal, Argentina's small corn crop being the only exception.[3]

The year of 1913 saw production and trade increasing in Germany, France and England. Reports of particular industries, such as coal and iron, and figures of bank clear-

[1] *Mineral Industry*, vol. xxii, p. 384.

[2] *Ibid.*, p. 125.

[3] *Bureau of Crop Estimates*, Dept. of Agriculture, 1913.

ings, gross earnings of railroads, and volume of bills of exchange, all indicate an increase in domestic production, even though at a somewhat retarded rate.[1] In Germany, industrial activity slackened sporadically and, in particular industries, there were symptoms of overproduction. Building and related industries decreased in activity, because of the untoward conditions of the investment market. The reports of the electro-technical, metal, machine, and textile industries showed tendencies toward inactivity, but the production trend was not downward. Pig iron and coal production continued to advance throughout the year. Germany's foreign trade became very striking in its trend. Imports remained fairly constant, but exports gained decidedly, exceeding, for the first time, 10 billion marks. Her unfavorable balance of trade diminished from $413 million, in 1912, to $147 million, in 1913. Her exports gained chiefly in agricultural, mineral, and manufactured products, especially those of the mining, electro-chemical, machine and textile industrials, where the influence of the Kartells was felt most.

France gave evidence of a healthy industrial activity, during the first half of 1913, but the second half saw a recession of this activity, owing, partly, to bad crops, and partly to a stringency in money that developed out of the increase of her unfavorable balance of foreign trade, from $293 to $398 million. France's exports of foods and raw materials decreased, while those of manufactured articles increased only moderately. Imports gained in all commodities, but chiefly in manufactured articles. Because of the French investments in the Balkans, the iron and steel trades were occupied during the first half of the year with war orders from those countries, and war preparations at home added to

[1] *Cf. Volkswirtschaftliche Chronik*, 1913, pp. 901 *et seq.*

the activity. But during the second half-year there was a serious falling off in the demand.[1]

Production and trade in England followed very much the same course as it did in Germany. Signs of slackening occurred only in the last half of the year, these being evident in a diminishing rate of increase rather than in actual decrease, and the total physical volume was maintained. Coal and pig-iron production show great advances, though, as a whole, iron and steel manufacturers found the year less satisfactory. The cotton and wool manufacturers reported gains. The foreign trade of England increased the first half year but declined in the second. The unfavorable trade balance was reduced from $708 million, in 1912, to $651 in 1913. Exports of raw materials and manufactured articles made the greatest gain, especially the textiles, shipping, and iron and steel products. Increases occurred in all articles of import, except for a slump in raw cotton and grain in the last half of the year. The increase in export of capital in the form of merchandise, coinciding with a contraction of trade with continental countries and a greater expansion of that with Colonial possessions, was the characteristic feature of British foreign trade during 1913.[2]

Employment Conditions in Europe. Unemployment statistics further testify to the course of business conditions in Europe. In Germany they indicate an increasing number of unemployed, a situation similar to that which existed in 1908-09. England experienced fewer labor difficulties, and, consequently, shows a better employment rate, though unfavorable tendencies developed in the latter half of 1913. The French statistics seem to indicate a state of considerable industrial activity during the first half of the year, but

[1] *London Economist*, vol. lxxvii, pp. 760-1 and 894.

[2] *Ibid.*, p. 54.

point to a relaxation in the demand for labor during the last half. In this respect, conditions in France correspond with those in Germany and England. It must be observed that, in Germany, unemployment was greater than elsewhere, largely as a result of peace in the Balkans, and the readjustment in the industries of continental countries, which followed:

UNEMPLOYMENT IN GERMANY, FRANCE AND ENGLAND [1]

1912	*Germany*	*France*	*England*
Jan.	2.9%	8.2%	2.7%
May	1.9	5.5	2.7
Aug.	1.5	5.4	2.2
Oct.	1.8	5.1	1.8
1913			
Jan.	3.2	6.4	2.2
May	2.5	4.7	1.9
Aug.	2.8	4.9	2.0
Oct.	2.8	4.3	2.2

The labor market in Germany was perturbed by an increasing number of strikes and lockouts, during 1913. Building and related trades, moreover, diminished in activity, and, in the latter part of the year, some unemployment was reported in the electro-technical, textile, metal, and machine industries. In addition, the labor market evidenced an oversupply because of the great immigration of labor. These factors account to some degree for the high unemployment rate in Germany, in spite of the industrial expansion during 1913.

Credit and Investment Conditions. The demand for funds for commercial and investment purposes, in the United States, was manifested in a financial strain that developed in the latter part of 1912 and continued throughout the greater part of 1913. Although no such acute strain as

[1] *Cf. supra*, p. 48, for sources of unemployment statistics.

that of 1907 occurred, the tension nevertheless was more persistent. Because of the liquidation in the security market and the depletion of reserves, New York clearing-house banks contributed their loans during the latter half of 1912. These loans increased, however, early in 1913, and remained on a slightly higher level of volume, during most of that year.[1] Total loans of all national banks expanded during the first part of 1913, but during the summer and fall months, except for a brief financing of crops, there was a moderate contraction.

The following figures indicate the loans and deposits of the two groups of banks:

	All National Banks (in million dollars)		New York Clearing House Banks		
	Loans, etc.	*Individual Deposits*	*Average for*	*Loans, etc.*	*Deposits*
1912					
Nov. 26	$6.085	$5.946	Nov.	$1.281	$1.252
1913					
Feb. 4	6.147	5.987	Feb.	1.376	1.385
Apr. 4	6.198	5.972	Apr.	1.335	1.331
June 4	6.162	5.955	June	1.321	1.338
Aug. 9	6.187	5.763	Aug.	1.364	1.376
Oct. 21	6.288	6.053	Oct.	1.351	1.337

The contraction of loans for production purposes during 1913 was offset by credit requirements of mercantile and agricultural classes; moreover, heavy demands for investment funds helped to prevent bank loans from declining for the year.

The investment market was subject to a severe strain and congestion in 1913. New issues of securities, as shown by the listings, were large. Bonds reached the total of the previous year with $447 millions, though stocks receded from $463 to $264 millions. Railroads and public utilities

[1] *Cf. supra,* pp. 133 *et seq.*

made heavy security offerings, those of the railroads being the result of a serious impairment of credit due to the decline in earnings during the last six months, to advances in wages, and to the postponement of rate increases. Furthermore, the money stringency that existed made railroad borrowing precarious. To illustrate, the Milwaukee and St. Paul issue of $30 millions general mortgage bonds at 4½ per cent sold poorly. The Baltimore and Ohio offer of $63 millions at 4½ per cent was untouched by the shareholders at 95½ and the syndicate dissolved with $47 millions left on hand, having paid 92½ and sold to the public at 91⅞. The railroads, therefore, resorted to short-term obligations on a 6 to 6½ per cent basis. Industrial corporations, municipalities, and states were also forced into this method of financing because of their inability to float stocks or long-time bonds, and because they could rely somewhat upon the elasticity of bank loans. The exclusion of American security offers from the European investment markets was the result largely of the prevailing dearth of capital abroad.

As a result of high interest rates and the strained condition of the investment market, building operations fell off. The monthly value of building permits issued by the 20 selected cities, heretofore quoted, indicates the degree of recession:

	1912	*1913*
	($100,000.)	
1st quarter	$1.086	$1.116
2nd quarter	1.802	1.544
3rd quarter	1.381	1.228
4th quarter	1.264	1.099
Total	5.541	4.987

In Europe the capital market felt a manysided strain. The fair amount of industrial development maintained during the year, characterized by considerable advances in some spheres, resting largely upon favorable agricultural conditions, required additional capital. Capital losses resulting from wars and the use of capital in preparations for war, the crisis in China, in Argentina, and in Brazil, the revolution in Mexico, and the presentiment of a world war, all these drained the market of funds. Heavy taxes and the high costs of living, together with extensive hoarding, on the other hand, stopped the inlets to the reservoir of funds.[1] The countries bordering the Balkans were most affected. There were runs on the banks of Austria-Hungary as a result of the apprehension of war felt generally. The Balkans had freely bought Austrian manufactures, but their continued moratorium reacted adversely upon Austrian credits and industry. This reaction spread also to Germany. On account of these political disturbances, the French, especially, began hoarding and even refused to lend to their old clients.

This perilous state of the investment markets in continental Europe caused a rush to London to obtain capital. The underwriters on the continent had on hand, by the end of 1912, many undigested securities, a dead-weight upon the market. In Germany the total issues were exactly equal in volume to those of 1912.[2] The domestic issues declined $88 millions, while the foreign issues increased by that much. Bond floatation gained $57 millions, while a corresponding decrease occurred in stocks, especially in industrials. The issues of home governments increased $50

[1] Estimated Costs of Wars and Armaments by the *London Economist* places the cost of the Balkan struggle at approximately $1,250,000,000. Roumania spent $60,000,000 on mobilization and armaments from Nov., 1912 to July, 1913. Austria-Hungary and Russia spent $200,000,000 for the same purpose, while Germany administered a capital levy of $250,000,000 for war budgets and France $125,000,000. *Cf. Chronicle*, vol. xcvii, pp. 198 and 327.

[2] *Cf. supra*, p. 123.

millions and those of foreign states, $104 millions over 1912. The latter appeared in a larger amount than in any year since 1905; their issue was taken over by the German banks from political motives.[1] A large number of the foreign securities issued were Chinese, Roumanian and Austrian. The stringency in the French investment market was evident in the high official rates of discount maintained. Foreign issues diminished, while the internal demands for new capital were great. The total issues, in 1913, were $966 million as compared with $989 million, in 1912. Stocks, chiefly industrials, came forward strongly, with $454 million, and bonds, with $335 millions, as compared with $558 millions of stocks, and $284 millions of bonds, in 1912. In England, the demands for new capital were greater during the first half of 1913 than they had been in the corresponding period of the previous year, and less in the second half. This was characteristic also of Germany and France. The new security issues were $956 millions, $70 millions less than in 1912. The English colonials, Canadian, and foreign issues, were the largest. Canada stood in the first rank in demands for capital, followed in order by England, Australia, the United States, Brazil, and Argentina. These issues remained largely in the portfolios of English financial institutions.[2] It is estimated that first-class issues were carried to the extent of 50-95 per cent.[3] Even though many of these securities were paid for by commodity exports, the congestion in the great credit institutions of England had a far-reaching effect in the money market. The necessity for financing large crops in India and Egypt caused rates to mount still higher in London.

[1] *Cf. Volkswirtschaftliche Chronik*, 1913, p. 963.

[2] *Cf. ibid.*, 1913, p. 980.

[3] This is the estimate given by the *London Bankers' Magazine*.

British investors were restrained by these high money rates, as well as, by the oversupply of unabsorbed securities, and new flotations met with even less demand from investors, because security values were declining on stock exchanges, the world over.[1] The struggle of continental banks for gold further drained the English market. France could not come to the rescue, because of the hoarding prevailing there, and because of her undertaking to supply the needs of the Balkans for funds. The result was the failure of one issue after another and the suspension of enterprises far and wide for the want of funds.

Profits and Commercial Failures. This great demand for capital arrayed itself with high price of materials, and mounting costs of living with its usual train of labor unrest, to increase the cost of doing business to the point of causing the inevitable increase in commercial failures. In spite of this, profits in industry were good during the first part of 1913. In Germany the net income of 4.773 joint stock companies, and of 408 joint stock banks, show an increase for the year ending June 30, 1913, but a decrease during the last half of 1913 and first half of 1914.[2] Profits on capital, as shown by the investigation of 933 companies by the *London Economist,* indicate an increase for the year of from 8.5 per cent, in 1912, to 10.2 per cent, in 1913. Monthly figures, however, show a decline for the latter part of 1913. Profit statistics for the United States, in so far as they are available for that period, offer similar conclusions as to the decreasing returns of business, in the last six months of the year. Failures as reported by Bradstreet's seem to have been more prevalent during the latter half of 1913. The largest failures occurred in July, at

[1] *Cf. London Economist*, vol. lxxviii, p. 7.

[2] "Geschaftsergebnisse der Deutschen Aktien Gesellschaften" in the *Vierteljahrshefte zur Statistik des Deutschen Reichs.*

the time of the most acute stringency of money, and again in November and December, when the number of firms as well as the total of their liabilities was high.[1]

[1] In November some noted failures occurred, among them H. B. Hallens & Co., Wall Street Bank, Pope Manufacturing Co. and N. Y. Real Estate & Security Co.

CHAPTER VII

Causes of the Depression of 1913

The depression of 1913, in contrast to that of 1910-11, was universal.[1] But the reaction in the United States was perceptible at the very outset of the year, fully six months before the culmination of prosperity in Germany, France and England. It will be our task to discover the causes of this premature recession.

The Method Employed. Our problem in this instance presents many of the aspects of the foregoing one, concerning the depression of 1910-11, and we may base our analysis upon the same fundamental conception, namely, that business cycles are primarily credit phenomena. Business is directly motivated by prospective margins of profit. This motivation is accomplished principally through the medium of elastic bank credit, which in turn, influences the realization of these same prospective profits, through the price of credit—interest rates—and the diffusion of credit funds. The fact that prospective margins of profit are potential makes it necessary for business transactions to be projected into the future. This leads to a discounting of the future by the employment of credit to bridge over the production period. In times of business optimism, the consequent diffusion of circulating credit funds, arising out of excessive use of this elastic bank credit, foreshadowing an increasing demand, stimulates business activity and raises profits.

[1] *Cf. supra*, pp. 127-28.

This presaging of profits through the stimulating influences of credit, is the basis of business dynamics. Business expansion, based upon the increasing use of funds, can be carried forward only so far as elastic bank credit can be supplied,—irrespective, often, of such extraneous alterative factors as new markets, wars, good or bad crops, fortunes gleaned in mining, changes in technology of industry, and the like. This recurrent exhaustion of elastic bank credit is what gives business dynamics its rhythmic aspect.[1] Finally, the moment at which the supply of elastic bank credit becomes exhausted is determined by the extent to which funds have been disproportionately distributed, and by the intensity of business activity that has prevailed. Supply of bank credit, business activity and the manner in which funds are used, are themselves interdependent.

Accordingly, the factors in our problem may be stated as follows: First, what supply of banking funds was available at the beginning of business revival in the latter part of 1911, and what growth was there in the supply during 1912, as compared with the two preceding prosperity periods of 1904-07 and 1908-09? Second, in what manner were these funds employed during 1912? Third, to what degree was the spirit of business enterprise manifest during the year, as compared with the previous boom periods of 1904-07 and 1908-09? Fourth, to what extent did foreign factors undermine the credit and investment resources of this country.

Supply of Banking Funds Available. The banking resources of this country at the close of 1911 were not as equal to the requirements of the ensuing expansion as they had been just before the revivals of 1905 and 1909. The call-loan rates in New York reached their lowest figure in

[1] Discussion of this factor will appear in Chapter VIII.

August 1910, at 1.55 per cent, while throughout the greater part of 1911, they remained in the neighborhood of 2.30 per cent. These rates are higher than those of August 1904 and 1908, which stood at .90 per cent and 1.06 per cent, respectively. The same degree of difference is to be noted between 60-90 day paper rates. The lowest rate prevailed in May 1911, at 3.63 per cent, and, again, only 3.75 per cent, in February of 1912, having been subject to an increase in the autumn of 1911. These rates may be seen to be high in comparison to the figures reached in the depressions of 1904 and 1908, when they stood at 3.55 per cent and 3.61 per cent, respectively.[1] New York clearing house banks' reserves were lower than those of 1908. The largest total in June 1911 was $401 millions, and $402 in February 1912, while in 1908, the figure was $407 millions. Nor were the reserve ratios of these banks as favorable in the period under discussion. In June 1911, the pecentage was 28.09, and in February 1912, 27.14, while the highest ratio of 1908 reached in August, was 29.69 per cent, and of August 1904, 29.61 per cent. Ratios of cash reserves to net deposits of all National banks indicate a similar situation. On June 7, 1911, the ratio was only 16.1 per cent as compared with 18.6 per cent, on May 14, 1908, and 18.1 per cent on June 9, 1904.[2] Such statistical compilations as that of the *Review of Economic Statistics* corroborate the figures given above.

[1] *Cf. supra*, pp. 84-86.

[2] It might be suggested that the basis for comparing the reserve ratios of all National banks over a period of time is not sufficiently homogeneous. For the legal requirements of reserves for the three classes of banks differ and the shifting of reserves between the classes would affect the potential loaning capacity of the banks. A shifting of reserves from the reserve cities to the country banks would increase the available supply of bank credit, just as if the total reserves had been actually increased.

Furthermore, there was no sudden upbuilding of bank reserves in 1910-11, such as had occurred in 1904 and 1908; consequently the possibility of supplying business with elastic bank credit was greatly reduced. The minimum requirements too, during the depression of 1910-11, were rather high, for there had been a fair volume of business, and moderately high prices. It may be seen from these conditions that the surplus of banking resources in 1911 was smaller than it had been in either 1904 or 1908. This fact, however, loses some of its significance when we remember that the business depression in industrial and investment circles in 1910-11 was not so severe as that of 1903-04 and 1908.[1]

Increase in Bank Reserves during 1912. The favorable gold balance of the year 1911 made possible an accretion to the bank reserves upon which business could rely in 1912. Following the almost perfect balance between imports and exports of gold in 1910, when the heavy losses of 1908-09 had ceased, there was an excess of imports amounting, in 1911, to $20 millions and, in 1912, to $19 millions.[2] This betterment in the gold situation brought about a gradual increase again in the monetary stock of the country, an increase that had been interrupted during 1908, 1909 and part of 1910.[3] The increase in bank reserves, however, which, as we have stated, was made possible by the favorable balance of gold, was only moderate.[4] All

[1] Ratios of reserves of New York clearing house banks during depressions:

Nov., 1902 to July, 1904—26.76%
Jan., 1908 to Sept., 1908—28.44
Jan., 1910 to Dec., 1911—26.81

[2] To this increase must be added the domestic gold production of about $95 millions annually, minus about $40 millions going to industrial use.

[3] *Cf. supra*, p. 43.

[4] Following is a comparison of the percentages of increase or decrease

National banks showed an increase from 1910 to 1911, of 7 per cent, whereas the increase in 1912 over 1911 was only 2.8 per cent. In 1913, there was an actual decrease of 2.2 per cent. Nor were reserves replenished to the same extent as they were in 1903-04 and 1907-08, for reason that gold accumulation was less in 1910-11, than in 1903-04 and 1908-09,[1] and that the depression was less severe in 1910-11, than it was in 1903-04 and 1908. The result was a narrower margin in the degree of elasticity present in bank credit, before the boom of 1912 set in, and surplus banking resources insufficient to support a prolonged business expansion.

Turning to a consideration of the supply of foreign funds, upon which American business was in the habit of depending, to a greater or less extent, according to requirements as they arose, we find those funds to a large degree unavailable in 1913, and, in addition, even a withdrawal of funds by Europe. The reasons for this situation were similar to those which prevented American borrowing there in 1909 except that they were more pronounced.[2] We

in cash reserves of all National banks during the three periods in question:

1903–04	—Increase—	16.8%
1904–07	"	6.7
1907–08	"	23.7%
1908–09	"	1.7
1909–10	—Decrease—	2.9
1910–11	—Increase—	7.0%
1911–12	"	2.8
1912–13	—Decrease—	2.2

[1] Accumulations to total gold stock in the United States:

1904–07 =	$398 millions.
1908–09 =	33 "
1910–11 =	197 "

Figures taken from the *Reports of the Director of the Mint.*

[2] *Cf. supra*, pp. 102-103.

will make a more detailed study of them in subsequent pages.[1]

Use and Distribution of Funds during 1912. The business expansion of 1912 affords a novel contrast to other periods of growing activity, in that, speculative dealings in the security market were a negligible factor.[2] Production and trade, on the other hand, show a vigorous growth, in spite of moderately rising prices. During most of the two years of depression, 1910 and 1911, stock prices had fluctuated about a fairly even level; but, in the fall of the latter year, they began to advance slowly. Railroad stocks did little more than hold their own in 1912, even the railroad earnings were very good. The explanation of this depression seems to lie in the continuous liquidation in rail stocks accomplished by foreign holders. Due to the large issues of new bonds thrown upon the market in 1912, and to the stringency that obtained in credit, bonds receded sharply in price. Industrials were the only securities that made a real advance in price, and these rose only moderately. The volume of sales of stocks remained very low, and evidence of the striking absence of speculative interest in the market. Now issues of stocks broke all previous records.[3] This fact, together with the large new issues of bonds, gave rise to a marked congesion of unabsorbed securities in the investment market, and in the portfolios of financial houses. Following is a table showing the comparative activity from 1910 to 1912 inclusive, of activity in the security market, and also a comparison among the periods 1904-07, 1908-09 and 1911-12;[4]

[1] *Cf. supra*, pp. 170-171.

[2] *Cf. supra*, p. 107.

[3] *Cf. supra*, p. 122, for figures of listings on New York stock exchange.

[4] Compare this table with that on page 91.

RELATIVE FIGURES—1903 = 100

Year	Price of 12 Industrial Stocks	Price of 20 Railroad Stocks	Volume of security sales on N. Y. Stock Exchange		Volume of new listings on N. Y. Stock Exchange	
			No. of Shares	Par value of bonds	Par value of Stocks	Par value of Bonds
1910.......	152	114	102	87	179	300
1911.......	148	114	79	116	148	208
1911 4th qt.	142	112	...	...	...	...
1912.......	158	116	81	95	268	233
1912 3rd qt.	163	118	...	...	...	...

COMPARISON OF PERIODS—1904-07; 1908-09; 1911-12

(PER CENT OF INCREASE OR DECREASE IN ABOVE ITEMS DURING EACH PERIOD)

(THE MINIMUM AND MAXIMUM QUARTER YEARS ARE TAKEN AS BASIS OF FIGURES)

Period	Per cent	Months	Per cent	Months	Per cent	Years	Per cent	Years	Per cent	Years	Per cent	Years
1904 to 07	94	27	38	36	76	3	—59 (dec.)	2	67	2	196	2
1908 to 09	70	24	41	21	12	1	120	2	100	1	243	2
1911 to 12	21	9	6	9	2	1	—21 (dec.)	1	120	1	25	1

It is evident from these figures that, except for a fair advance in the price of industrials, and the heavy listings of new stocks, the security market remained practically inactive during this period. A partial reason for this inactivity, as compared with the situation in 1904-07 and in 1908-09, may be assigned to the fair amount of business activity that was maintained in 1910-11. Moderate business profits, together with a reasonable price of credit, kept the market from sinking to so low a level of depression as it had in the two previous periods. The extent, therefore, to which prices and dealings in securities could increase during 1912, was restricted. Therefore, the maximum of advancement in prices and volume of sales, in 1912, were below those of 1906-07 and 1909, the two preceding periods of culmination of prosperity.

Commensurate with this moderate activity in the security market, was the mild expansion of loans and discounts of the New York clearing-house banks. This index of the use of credit indicates a small increase, compared with the boom periods of 1904-07 and 1908-09. The surplus reserves of these banks declined rapidly in 1912, so that on November 28, there was a deficit of over $5 millions. The reserve ratio, also, decreased from an average of 27.33 per cent for January to 25.33 per cent, for November, and cash holdings diminished by $78 millions, during the same period. The result was a heavy strain on the inadequate banking resources, followed by a sharp advance in the price of credit. 60-90 day paper rose from approximately 4 per cent, in July, to 6 per cent in October, while call loan rates increased from an average of 2.48 per cent, for July, to 6.50 per cent, for December.[1] With the exception of a temporary relaxation in January and February, this high price for credit was maintained throughout 1913. Owing to the fair degree of activity on the stock exchange all through 1910-11, there remained only a narrow margin of surplus reserves in the New York clearing-house banks, and the supply of bank credit was therefore too meagre to support any outstanding advance in the security market. We cannot avoid the conclusion that the culmination of activity in the security market, in the fall of 1912, was the result of depleted bank credit available for that market, and of rapidly climbing interest rates. Funds were also withdrawn from the market to be employed in commercial and industrial undertakings.

Following is a summary of the extent to which bank credit was available for the security market during 1912, as compared with the periods of 1904-07 and 1908-09;

[1] It might be marked that the actual price of credit equals interest rates plus bank commissions.

NEW YORK CLEARING HOUSE BANKS *

RELATIVE FIGURES—1903 = 100

Year	Loans and Discounts	Net Deposits	Reserves	Reserve Ratios
1910	145	135	136	26.70 %
1911	147	153	156	26.91
4th qt.	147	150	147	25.49
1912	151	155	153	26.04
1st qt.	155	162	165	26.75
4th qt.	144	144	138	25.36

* Compare this table with that on page 95

COMPARISON OF PERIODS—1904-07; 1908-09; 1910-11

THE DEGREE OF EXPANSION OF ITEMS IN PERCENTAGE, FROM THE MINIMUM TO THE MAXIMUM QUARTERS OF THE FIRST AND LAST YEAR RESPECTIVELY, AND ALSO THE DECREASE OF RESERVES

Periods	Inc. %	Months	Inc. %	Months	Inc. %	Months	Decrease %	Months
1904-07	24	9	38	9	50	9	37	15
1908-09	19	12	38	21	71	9	39	12
1911-12	8	3	12	3	18	3	27	9

An analysis of these comparative figures gives evidence of the fact that elastic bank credit reached its limit of expansion very rapidly in 1912. The margin of elasticity was narrow to begin with, and, owing to the fact that reserves of the New York banks lessened rapidly throughout 1912, the use of funds in the security market met with early restrictions. To obtain a more complete comprehension of the nature of this financial strain which developed in 1912 and the reasons therefor, we must carry our inquiry still further,—into conditions that made necessary the utilization of credit resources in the commercial and industrial fields.

The aforementioned activity in production and trade, that was maintained in moderation during 1910-11, received impetus from various sources in the late months of 1911, and was carried vigorously forward during 1912.[1] Production in all fields made remarkable advances, which continued,

[1] *Cf. supra*, pp. 115-118.

after a slight retardation in rate at the close of 1912, well into 1913. The following index numbers of production indicate the degree of industrial activity in 1912 and serve as a comparison between that of 1904-07 and 1908-09, and the former period. The index numbers of production compiled by W. W. Stewart check closely with other criteria of general production, and are presented below as representative:

INDEX NUMBERS OF PRODUCTION *

(AVERAGE PRODUCTION 1911-13 = 100)

Years	*All Commodities*	*Total Materials*	*Farm Materials*	*Minerals*	*Total Manufacture*
1903	75	83	86	64	68
1907	89	90	89	86	91
1908	84	91	95	79	78
1909	94	95	95	87	96
1911	93	93	93	93	92
1912	106	109	111	101	104
1913	101	98	96	106	104

* *American Economic Review*, vol. xi, p. 68.

INCREASE OF PRODUCTION IN PER CENT FOR 1903-07; 1908-09; 1911-12

1903-07 (Years—4)	14%	7%	3%	22%	23%
1908-09 (Years—1)	10%	4%	0%	8%	18%
1911-12 (Years—1)	13%	16%	18%	8%	12%

Additional data are given below as corroboration. These figures are used, also, in comparing similar data for 1903-07 and 1908-09. In order to keep the basis of comparison the same as that used on page 94, the averages for the half year periods in 1903 and 1904 have been retained as a base for the relative figures.

Year	*Bank Clearings Outside of N. Y.*	*Pig Iron Production*	*Building Permits*	*Imports*
1910	154	154	172	157
1911	156	134	171	154
1912	169	167	177	185

COMPARISON OF PERIODS 1904-07; 1908-09; 1911-12

ERCENTAGES INDICATING INCREASE IN ITEMS FROM MINIMUM TO MAXIMUM HALF-YEARS OF EACH PERIOD WITH THE MINIMUM FIRST HALF-YEAR OF 1904 AS THE BASE—EXCEPT FOR BUILDING PERMITS

1904 first half minimum	100	100	*1903* second half minimum 100	*1904* first half minimum 100
1911 first half minimum	159	144	200	150
1912 second half maximum	178	195	third and second quarter maximum 233	183
1911–12	19%—1½ years	51%—1½ years	33%—1⅓ years	33%—1½ years
1908–09	34 —1½ years	105 —1½ years	88 —1 year	46 —1 year
1904–07	24 —3 years	66 —3 years	73 —2½ years	47 —3 years

In comparing the percentages of increase in production during the three boom periods, we find that the degree and rapidity of expansion between the minimum and maximum of production were greater in 1911-12 than in the two previous periods. It is true that this conclusion is not supported by the comparative figures of bank clearings, pig iron production, building permits, and imports, but it must be remembered that bank clearings in 1912 were not influenced by a sharp rise in prices, characteristic of the other periods. Building permits, however, were considerably fewer in 1912 because construction was unfavorably affected by the strain in the investment market. Nevertheless, we may fairly state this conclusion, that production in 1912 was greater than the yearly average in 1904-07, while the production of materials, farm and mineral, was greater than in 1908-09. It was in the field of manufacture, however, that the growth in production of 1912 fell below that of 1908-09. Evidences point to the fact that this smaller production was the result largely of curtailment in construction. Again, it is necessary to recall that the contraction in the volume of production and trade was considerably less in the period of depression of 1910-11, than it had been in 1903 and 1908. Therefore, the resiliency of markets and capacity for production had been taken advantage of, to some extent, before the impetus for business expansion, in the beginning of 1912, got under way. Even though the production of manufactures was greater in 1908-09, it was more than offset in 1912, by the rapid increase in the production of minerals; and there is sufficient evidence that, on the whole, production increased relatively more in 1912 than in 1904-07.

The extent to which the pronounced production activity utilized bank credit in 1912 can be determined only by a study of the combined statements of all national banks. These are the only available bank credit data. The following tables indicate not only the credit expansion during 1912, and the relative expansion in 1904-07 and 1908-09, but, also, the relative increase in general wholesale prices:

RELATIVE FIGURES—1890-99 = 100

	ALL NATIONAL BANKS				U. S. BUREAU OF LABOR
Years	*Loans and Discounts*	*Individual Deposits*	*Cash Reserves*	*Reserve Ratio*	*Wholesale Commodity Index*
1910......	264	296	223	15.2%	131.6 (Max. March=133.8)
1911......	273	304	238	15.4	129.2 (Min. May =128.1)
1912......	290	327	246	14.9	133.6 (Max. Nov. =135.4)
1913......	301	336	243	14.3	135.2 (Max. Nov. =135.8)

SUMMARY COMPARISON

Period	*Increase in per cent*			*No. of years*	*Per cent increase*
1904-1907........	47	48	11	3	20.8 (Oct., 1904-Oct., 1907)
(1907-08)........	..	..	(44)	1	...
1908-09..........	19	28	4	1	10.8 (Aug., 1908-Dec., 1909)
1911-12..........	17	23	8	1	7.3 (May, 1911-Nov., 1912)

NOTE.—National banks' holdings of non-government bonds and stocks increased strikingly, $203 millions, during 1911 and 1912.

The use of bank credit in the increasing industrial activity during 1912 was almost commensurate with that of 1908-09, and greater than that in 1904-07,—judging by average yearly increase.

The rise in general wholesale prices was not as great as in 1908-09, largely because of the moderate price level maintained during the depression of 1910-11. The increase in physical volume of production, however, was proportionately more than the increase in prices. Therefore, at the close of 1912, business required the maximum amount of credit that banking resources could supply. The effect of this pressure of business expansion upon the supply of bank credit may be seen in the fact that reserve ratios of all national banks declined during 1912 and 1913, reaching a level lower than any arrived at hitherto. The great demand for funds, made by commercial and industrial interests, drew heavily upon the supply available for stock-exchange dealings and for the security market in general. Hence the decline in the security market during the autumn of 1912, and the congestion of the investment market, because of unabsorbed securities, indicated by the heavy increase in holdings of private securities by national banks. Also, as we have previously indicated, the volume of dealings in securities on the stock exchange was not nearly commensurate with the heavy new flotations of stocks and bonds.[1] Considerable funds, therefore, were tied up in unliquid investments by financial institutions. Security issues, to obtain working capital, were evidently the last resort of business enterprises, for bank credit could no longer be supplied by the banking community. The sudden and marked increase in interest rates during the third quarter of 1912, and the unusually prolonged continuation of these high rates throughout 1913, offer incontestable evidence of the paucity of bank credit during these years.

The usual factors that increase the demand for credit, during periods of cumulation of prosperity, were clearly

[1] *Cf. supra*, p. 156.

present in the closing months of 1912.[1] In addition, the abundant crop yields, with the consequent extraordinary demand for funds, became a dominating factor in the credit market. Furthermore, the sharp demands of Europe for funds involved extensive selling of foreign-held securities and the recalling of foreign loans from the American market. Such European demands, however, were offset largely by the export credits obtained through huge cotton and grain exports in the fall of 1912. These credits were more than sufficient, for the large favorable trade balance resulted in a considerable amount of gold imports.

Financial strain developed suddenly in the early part of the fall of 1912 and the price of credit rose violently. Our rather inelastic credit system, functioning upon a bare minimum of reserves, had become so expanded, and our bank portfolios had become so congested with unmarketable securities and loans upon securities, as to generate stresses in the investment and credit markets. Exorbitant interest rates and the extensive liquidation of securities on foreign account undermined the prices of securities and caused the collapse of the market in August and October. A rapid depletion of the reserves of the New York clearing house banks
production and trade generally. However, inability to ob-
was accomplished during the latter part of 1912, and led to a deficit in November. This strain in the credit market did not exert a depressing influence upon commodity prices,
tain funds by means of new security issues, and the undermining of loans upon security collateral by decline in the prices of stocks and bonds, affected those industries dealing in raw materials and producers' goods as early as January, 1913. The decline in contruction had become

[1] These factors are rising costs, prime and supplementary, increasing volume of business and rising prices.

exceedingly marked during the last half of 1912, because of the unfavorable conditions prevailing in the investment market. In January, 1913, this was reflected in the sharp recession of unfilled orders of the United States Steel Corporation, and of a break in copper and cotton prices, which occurred also at this time. Certain favorable factors combined, nevertheless, to keep industry in a relatively prosperous condition, far into 1913, yet even these tended more and more to increase the financial strain, that continued unremittingly throughout 1913. The primary factors were: (a) The abundant crops, which augmented the consuming power of the agricultural classes and rendered the railroads more prosperous. A sharp impetus to the price of grain resulted from grain speculation; this speculation being due to the possible exclusion, from the market, of the Russian crop, owing to the impending Balkan war, and the restriction of the European bank credits upon which the movement of those crops depended. (b) Good employment conditions and a tardy increase in wages together with continuing large, though declining, profits in industries. This was the result chiefly of the large volume of contracts that remained to be filled after the short and active boom of 1912. There was a sharp decrease in the volume of business after the first six months of 1913.

The stringency of credit would have been more severe if the huge exports of cotton and grain, previously referred to, had not led to an importation of gold during the fall of 1912,[1] lasting until January, 1913, when the heavy outflow was resumed.[2] The consequence of this return to former

[1] Some outright purchases of gold in the London market were executed by New York bankers in October, 1912. *Cf. Commmercial and Financial Chronicle*, vol. xcvi, pp. 35-9.

[2] The net exports of gold during the first six months of 1913 equalled $35,824,000. *Cf. New York Times*, August 30, 1914, Chas. A. Conant, "How Financial Europe prepared for the Great War."

conditions was a further impairment of banking resources and the continuance of high interest rates. This prolonged monetary stringency interacted with the liquidating process, which was initiated when prices began to fall during the early months of 1913. The price level declined only moderately during the year, but the ensuing business readjustment levied a heavy toll of commercial failures toward the end.

The depression in Europe was postponed until the close of 1913, because of the better position there of banking resources and investment funds, these in turn being the result of efficient and resilient credit systems. The wider markets for European industries also sustained business prosperity for about six months longer than it lasted in the United States.

The Causes of the Depression of 1913. The intricate complexity of economic forces that underlie business dynamics will not permit us, at this time, any detailed study of the interrelated causes that produce the business cycle. We must accept the hypothesis that depressing influences upon business may usher in a period of liquidation at a time when elastic bank credit has reached its maximum expansion, and we shall content ourselves with an attempt at explanation of the outstanding factors that produced, in the United States, the premature reaction of 1913 without, necessarily, any inquiry into the nature of the multifarious circumstances that are involved in a study of business cycles.

Let us consider, then, what were the factors that undermined the credit and investment resources of this country. First among the more important of these was the diminution in rate of increase of the gold supply following 1908, with the continuing urgency of requirements for credit and funds. Although additions did occur in our gold supply, except in 1909 and 1910, the rate of increase in reserves was not at all commensurate with that of the demand for funds required by our economic growth and the activity of our investment enterprise.

The gold position of the United States as compared with Europe is indicated by the following figures:

RELATIVE FIGURES—1890-99 = 100

	GERMANY		FRANCE		ENGLAND		UNITED STATES	
Year	*Gold Balance*	*Reserves of Reichsbank*	*Gold Balance*	*Reserves of Bank of France*	*Gold Balance*	*Reserves of Bank of England*	*Gold Balance*	*Cash holdings of National Banks*
1904	+ 492	106	+ 528	123	+ 12	111	— 581	171
1905	+ 228	111	+ 641	133	+ 117	114	+ 48	174
1906	+ 365	103	+ 267	132	+ 52	105	+ 1,758	171
1907	— 26	103	+ 287	123	+ 93	110	+ 1,419	182
1908	+ 392	121	+ 985	133	— 59	120	— 500	226
1909	+ 37	123	+ 179	152	+ 111	120	— 1,435	230
1910	+ 222	124	+ 56	143	+ 96	122		223
1911	+ 185	132	+ 123	135	+ 130	126	+ 323	238
1912	+ 256	134	+ 189	135	+ 92	128	+ 308	245
1913	+ 308	150	+ 581	133	+ 201	123	— 468	242

The above data indicates: (1) that the gold balances of Germany, France and England remained constantly favorable with the exception of 1907 for Germany, of 1908 for England; (2) that the accretions to reserves were greater in 1904-08 than in 1908-12 or -13;[1] (3) that the variability was extraordinary in the gold balance of the United States as well as in the scattered reserves of the national banks. The heavy gains in gold up to 1908, the subsequent heavy losses and the moderate additions following in 1911-12, together with another loss in 1913, all had significant effect

[1] The comparative percentage increase in reserves of the central banks of Europe and the National banks:

From	*Reichsbank*	*Bank of France*	*Bank of England*	*National Banks*
1904–1908	15%	10%	9%	55%
1908–1912	13%	2%	8%	19%
1908–1913	29%	0%	3%	16%

upon the basis for credit in the United States. The supply of gold thus became indeterminate, as well as insufficient in 1912, to meet the credit requirements for American business.

The reasons for the retarded growth in the gold accretions of the United States were twofold: first, the slower rate of increase in the world's gold production after 1908, and, second, the heavy intensely competitive demands for gold by European and other countries. The retarded rate of gold production is indicated by the following figures:

Relative Figures—1890-99 = 100

Average relative for five years:	1899-1903 = 147
" " " " "	1904-1908 = 202
" " " " "	1909-1913 = 234
	1908 = 225
	1909 = 231
	1910 = 231
	1911 = 235
	1912 = 237

The demands for gold, during the period of 1908-13 by European and other countries, arose from several sources. First, there was the universal business expansion. The extent of this expansion in Europe may be judged from the data below:

Relative Figures—1890-99 = 100

	GERMANY		FRANCE		ENGLAND	
Year	*Bank clearings*	*Gross earnings R. R-*	*Paris bank clearings*	*Gross earnings R. R.*	*London bank clearings*	*Gross earnings R.*
1904	153	148	199	119	143	125
1908	213	176	382	137	164	133
1913	343	231	521	162	223	148
Increase:						
1904-08	60%	28%	183%	18%	21%	8
1908-13	120%	55%	139%	25%	59%	15

The larger increase in volume of business during the latter period as compared with that of the preceding one, gave rise to a correspondingly greater need for credit.

Moreover, the rise in price level of these countries being relatively greater than it was in the period of 1904-07, the need for credit was further augmented. The comparative growth in the use of credit is presented by the following figures:

RELATIVE FIGURES—1890-99 = 100

	Reichsbank		Bank of France		Joint Stock Banks of England	
Year	*Note circulation*	*Loans and discounts*	*Note circulation*	*Loans and discounts*	*Deposits on current account*	*Loans and discounts*
1904	123	127	124	120	132	128
1908	146	150	141	142	147	140
1913	185	187	154	201	170	159
Increase:						
1904-08	23%	23%	17%	22%	15%	12%
1908-13	39%	37%	13%	59%	23%	19%

We have brought together, below, the totals of new security issues of all kinds during the two periods 1903-1907 and 1908-1912. These estimates are indicative of the huge applications for capital:

Years	*World*
Total for 5 years	
1903-07	$18.1 billions
1908-12	21.7 "

The heaviest increase in new securities issued from 1908 to 1911 occurred in England and France, where foreign applications figured prominently.

In addition to this universal business expansion, there arose certain other sources which may be assigned for the demands for gold. Military and political exigencies in Europe accentuated the desire of nations to procure larger supplies. The general apprehensions regarding the probability of a European war, immediately incited by the Balkan embroglio and the Moroccan controversy, induced extreme hoarding on the part of banks and individuals throughout Europe, a hoarding which, toward the close of

1912, assumed striking proportions.[1] In order to obtain gold, special inducements were offered. The Reichsbank, for example, assumed the interest charges on gold imports in transportation. France, as a result of her unfavorable balance of trade and heavy exportation of capital, in 1912 and 1913, resorted to outright purchases. Many special transactions were executed in New York by Paris, when foreign exchange rates did not warrant them. The Bank of France, to conserve the gold supply, asked a high premium for gold at the counter.

The consequence of this extraordinary call for gold was the impairment of the available supply for the United States, tending to jeopardize the basis for an adequate supply of bank credit, to sustain the business progress beyond 1912. The medium through which the restriction of gold acquisitions operated is to be found, of course, in the international balance sheet. The position of the United States as a debtor nation was a real handicap to the international competition for gold and funds. The large favorable trade balance maintained since the late 90's had been seriously curtailed in 1909 and 1910 and, although an increase occurred again in 1911 and 1912, it was not the growth commensurate with the degree of industrial expansion that the

[1] *Cf. supra*, p. 125—table on the decrease in the deposits of the German Joint Stock banks. Also *supra*, p. 67—note on German and French Savings banks. *Cf. Report of Reichsbank for 1912*—"The great and continuously progressive revival in economic affairs brought upon the banks a large demand for money and credit; enhanced through the fact that owing to the diminution of loans withdrawn from Germany in consequence of the Moroccan crisis left the German money market upon its own resources." Again—"Closely following the great demand for funds was the heavy calling in and hoarding of specie." *Cf. Volkswirtschaftliche Chronik*, 1912, p. 978.

Cf. Frankfurterzeitung, December 31, 1912, Official pressure was brought to bear upon European banks, directed toward a conservation of banking resources for military and political emergency.

country had undergone in the meantime.[1] This was caused chiefly by the more rapid development of industrial as compared with agricultural production.

The second factor to be considered, in the reduction of the credit and investment resources of the country, and therefore in the premature depression in 1913, is the withdrawal of foreign capital. The enormous demands for capital, the world over, during this period, sprang from many sources. The plethora of new security issues, public and private, weighed heavily upon the banking resources of all countries. The security markets also reacted sluggishly under the heavy strain upon investment funds, and the result was that the financial houses were burdened with unabsorbed securities. Hoarding, the impairment of the increase in the rate of savings,[2] and the heavy demands for commercial funds, left a large bulk of securities in the hands of investment institutions. Furthermore, mobility of banking funds was restricted because of the inability of banks to liquidate or shift investments through the security markets. The cash demands for capital may be classified thus: (1) those that arose from the cumulative development of resources in the colonial and economically undeveloped countries;[3] (2) those that directly or indirectly, by way of

[1] Excess of mdse. exports over imports of the United States (millions of dollars).

1904	$415	1908	$637
1905	448	1909	225
1906	477	1910	266
1907	500	1911	525
		1912	581

[2] *Cf. supra*, p. 67.

[3] *Cf. London Bankers Magazine*, vol. lxxxviii, p. 616. British capital investments in average percentages of four year periods:

	English	*Indian and Colonial*	*Foreign*
1901–04	52.5	30.0	17.5
1905–08	28.0	26.2	45.8
1909–12	18.2	33.8	48.0

preparations for hostilities, arose from the Balkan war, either out of the wastes of war or because of reconstruction purposes;[1] (3) those that were the result of the inauguration of governmental social programs, entered upon as a palliative to the discontent of the working classes, arising out of the high cost of living and the burden of heavy taxes;[2] (4) those that came of the industrial expansion resulting from the incentives of rising prices and increasing profits. In connection with this last factor, the increasing cost of business enterprises, due to the high prices of materials, added greatly to the volume of credit required.

The effect of this heavy demand for funds was felt in the continuous selling of foreign-held securities in the American market and in the recalling of loans by Europe. The shifting of foreign capital from the United States to other countries largely for purposes of developing new sources of raw materials and foodstuffs,—an activity occasioned by the high price of these commodities,—resulted inevitably in the serious curtailment of American borrowing abroad. Securities, especially, those of railroads, were regularly offered in the American market for the purpose of creating credits, or to procure gold for the settlement of balances in other countries in European account.

Considering the prosperity period of 1912 from the domestic standpoint, there was no evidence in the business situation to indicate an unhealthy development. The heavy issues of new securities did not represent so much an excessive promotion as they did a need for capital to meet the more or less normal expansion of industrial activity, which bank credit could not supply.

Finally, whatever stresses accumulated in the capital and

[1] *Cf. supra*, p. 146, note on Balkan war costs.

[2] In this connection the inauguration of a complete system of social insurance in England is a case in point.

credit markets of Europe were offset by greater economy in the use of credit resources. But this factor was again neutralized by the tendencies toward dissolution of the international money market, because of apprehensions of a possible war.[1] Thus these factors exerted little influence on the credit situation. The same cannot be said of the situation in the United States. Improvements in banking facilities and organization, which could have offset the lagging increase in gold for reserve purposes and the withdrawal of foreign capital, were practically negligible during these years.[2] What elasticity there was in our rather rigid credit system had become seriously impaired by industrial growth and the slow rate of increase in the monetary supply. Reserve ratios, oscillating within narrow limits, serve as an excellent illustration of this condition, which existed in our credit system from 1907 throughout the period under consideration. Expansion and contraction of bank credit, from 1909 to 1914, was possible only to a small extent and consisted largely in the necessary shifting of funds within the country as required. There seems to have been but a small degree of elasticity in the interior banks also, and as a result, the surplus reserves of the New York clearing-house banks underwent rapid depletion.[3] This is demonstrated by the conditions in 1909 and in 1912. To make matters more involved, the national bank note system, strikingly inelastic, required banks to meet the growing demands of the country for exchange media out of their cash holdings. Further-

[1] *Cf. supra*, pp. 134-138.

[2] The national banking act was not changed, and no fundamental alteration occurred in the practices of reserve holdings and in the check clearing system after 1908. However, the New York clearing house association did sanction a greater use of money other than gold in its clearing operations.

[3] This fact is evidenced by the declining reserve ratio of all national banks.

more, the congestion of the portfolios of banks with investment loans and securities, made it increasingly difficult for them to maintain the liquidity of loans.

Summary of Conclusions.

1. Owing to the retarded increase in reserves and the moderate volume of production and level of prices mantained in 1910 and 1911, the banking resources at the end of the period of depression of 1911 were not as ample as those during the two previous depressions of 1904 and 1908.

2. Since upbuilding of reserves during the foregoing depression had been less than in 1904 and 1908, the increase of reserves of banks was retarded during the prosperity period of 1912.

3. The security market became congested with new issues, the stock market remaining moderately active. Production and trade, on the other hand, increased greatly, drawing funds from the security market.

4. The investment and credit resources of the United States became seriously impaired, causing the depression in 1913, premature as compared with that of the European countries, and was due to the following factors:

a. The restricted acquisition of gold by the United States.

b. The withdrawal of foreign capital and loan funds.

c. The inefficient and inelastic nature of our credit system.

CHAPTER VIII

Varying Lengths of Cycles—Determining Factors

In re-evaluating the conclusions derived from our study of the causes of the two short business cycles between 1908 and 1913, we find considerable support for the belief that the margin of elasticity in the credit system limits the lengths of the cycles.

Elastic bank credit rests primarily upon reserves, while mercantile credit and, even to a considerable extent, long-time investment operations, are based upon bank credit. Bank reserves in turn are derived from and contain, from time to time, in part, the existing supply of capital, which means that a certain portion of the capital supply of a country is crystallized now and then in the form of bank reserves,—primarily, gold. This transmutation is accomplished directly, through the use of banking capital for the purpose of purchasing reserves, or, frequently, through the borrowing of gold, and, indirectly, through the depositing of reserve money by individuals and business enterprises and the repayment of loans and foreign exchange operations. Furthermore, credit resources may be directly affected by the flow of loan-funds, and indirectly by the flow of capital to and fro between nations.

By far the greater portion of a country's capital, however, exists in the form of business capital or productive wealth. Its potential purchasing power can be translated into means of payment only through the operations of bank credit based upon reserves. The connection, then, between that portion of a country's capital existing in the form of reserves and that part which exists in the shape of business capital, or productive wealth, is not far to seek. The latter requires its hand-maiden credit,—primarily bank credit,—to make it effective as a production agent and to make possible the flow of incomes and expenditures. It follows, that a country possessed of much capital is in a favorable position to obtain gold, and that this gold, serving as bank reserves, lays the basis for expansible bank credit, without which capital would remain relatively inert. Considered from the standpoint of its capital supply, a country is either capital-lending or capital-borrowing. It should be noted that the capital supply of a debtor country is greatly jeopardized from time to time.

It often happens that when there is a dearth of capital, government currency is often substituted for basic money, (usually gold) since specie money requires capital and labor for its production or obtainment. History abounds in such examples, which illustrate the necessity for an adjustment of the proportion between the quantum of business capital,—a highly variable fund of values,—and the supply of means of payment.

Banking power, in our modern credit economy, is a composite of the supply of bank reserves and the efficiency of their use. The total supply of capital in a country can be measured only by its value expressed in monetary units, and is registered from time to time in the earning capacity of capital in terms of money profits; while profits are regulated by the vicissitudes of the margin of credit elasticity within which prices and production oscillate. Thus, business capital becomes a highly nebulous thing, based as it is upon past, present and future earnings of productive wealth. The coining of its potential purchasing power, by means of credit, is equally variable, but remains within the well defined limits set by the margin of elasticity in bank credit. Elastic bank credit, built upon reserves is the predominant factor in regulating the earnings of business capital. In its function of enabling capital to be coined into circulating funds, it influences prices and production through the flow of incomes and expenditures. Regulating these, it determines the profitableness of capital investments upon the basis of its supply and price.

The margin of elasticity in the credit system has definable limits. The course of these limits is directed, on the one hand, by the approximate minimum of credit requirements in depressions when a low level of prices and production prevails and, on the other hand, by the expansibility of bank credit, determined by the variable quantum of capital kept in the form of bank reserves. The period 1908 to 1913 offers fairly convincing evidence that the contraction of the limits of credit elasticity was accountable for the two short cycles.

The Contraction of the Limits of Credit Elasticity and the Depressions of 1910-11 and 1913. Cogent illustrations of the principles here set forth are to be found in the period 1908 to 1913. We shall bring together briefly the chief factors, discussed in previous chapters, responsible for the increase in the minimum credit requirements for these years.

a. Growth of population, as a result of natural increase and through migration, was maintained at the usual rate (See Graph A p. 183).

b. The increase in the standrad of living made its slow and certain progress. Although real wages underwent a reduction from 1907 to 1912,[1] nevertheless, incomes of agricultural classes were augmented by the high prices of farm products. Profits, as indicated by the amount of dividend payments of industrial corporations, were very good.

[1] *Cf. Am. Econ. Rev.*, vol. xi, p. 421, Douglas and Lamberson, "The Movement of Real Wages 1890 to 1918."

c. Cost of living continued to rise rapidly during this whole period, a fact which led to universal complaint. Retail prices of goods show the following increase:

1890–99 = 100 *

1897 to 1903 = 15.0%
1903 to 1907 = 11.2%
1907 to 1913 = 29.8%

* Bureau of Labor Statistics weighted index.

d. The increase in costs of materials for business concerns was considerable. Especially was this true of farm products, which, according to the Census Reports, consumed 82 per cent of the total materials used by industries.[1]

Relative Wholesale Prices—1890–99 = 100 *

Points prices rose (+) or fell (—) in	*Raw Materials*	*Manufactures*	*Mineral Products*	*Farm Products*	*Animal Products*	*Farm Crops*
1897–1903	+35	+22	+36	+43	+29	+33
1903–1904	— 3	— 1	— 9	+ 5	— 4	+ 8
1904–1907	+13	+18	+22	+27	+22	+ 1
1907–1908	— 9	— 8	—19	—18	— 9	— 1
1908–1912	+21	+ 6	+14	+17	+20	+34

* Bureau of Labor Statistics.

The rapid development of mineral production and manufacturing, in comparison with the retarded growth in agricultural production,—a fact which we will discuss later,—was of utmost significance.

Index of Wholesale Prices—Bureau of Labor Statistics

relative figures—1913 = 100

Period	*Farm Products*	*Food, etc.*	*Cloths and Clothing*	*Fuel and Lighting*	*Metals and Metal Products*	*Building Materials*	*Chemicals and Dyes*	*House Furnishings*	*Miscellaneous*	*All Commodities*
1908	85	94	94	91	94	92	100	78	97	91
to										
1912	101	108	98	89	99	100	101	91	101	101
	+16	+14	+4	—2	+5	+8	+1	+13	+4	+10

Inc. (+)
Dec. (—)

e. The increase in wages for the period may be determined approximately by the index number of rates of wages per hour, and the index number of the decline in hours of work per week, as given by the Bureau of Labor Statistics:

RELATIVE FIGURES—1890–99 = 100

RATE OF WAGES PER HOUR	HOURS OF WORK PER WEEK
Increase in per cent	*Decrease in per cent*
1897 to 1903 = 17%	1897 to 1903 = 3.8%
1903 to 1904 = 1%	1904 to 1907 = 1.1%
1904 to 1907 = 13%	1908 to 1913 = 3.0%
1907 to 1908 = .4%	
1908 to 1913 = 18%	

The influence of trade-union development may be seen in this reduction of hours per week. Trade-union membership, from 1897 to 1903, increased from a half million to over two millions; from 1904 to 1908, it remained around two million, while from 1908 to 1913, the membership jumped to two and a half million.[1] From these figures, it would seem that the payrolls of business concerns required more money, because of higher wages paid.

f. Information as to changes in efficiency in production must remain purely impressionistic. It is a safe conjecture, however, that progress in efficiency was made especially in management and technological improvements.

g. Promotion and developmental work was fairly active throughout the period. There was also an enormous number of business combinations, and incorporations of business concerns assumed marked proportions. Capital underwent both intensive and extensive application. The large issues and the considerable residue of securities lodged in investment houses and banks attest this fact.

[1] *Cf. American Economic Review*, vol. xii, p. 45, George E. Barnett, "The Present Position of American Trade Unionism."

It seems evident from these factors, analyzed in greater detail in previous chapters, that, from 1908 to 1913, the level of minimum credit requirements was greatly increased. Just how much that increase rose above the normal growth of relatively permanent demands for credit is difficult to determine. The growth in population, increasing costs of maintaining and improving the standard of living, rapidly rising costs of materials and, to a lesser extent, of labor, and the extensive and intensive developmental work undertaken, raised the level of credit requirements. It is likely that progress in efficiency of production offset the above factors to some degree. But, if we admit the generally accepted theory that efficiency in production leads to expansion of production in order to provide for the unnecessaries which border more and more upon economically unproductive consumption, then it may be assumed that credit requirements remained about the same, whatever the influence of increased efficiency might have been. In spite of this, the conclusion that credit requirements rose can be safely drawn.

A brief summary may now be made of our previous conclusions regarding restriction upon the growth of elastic bank credit and upon the supply of foreign capital and loan-funds from 1908 to 1913:

a. Retardation occurred in the growth of banking reserves, owing to the slackening rate of gold production and the small acquisitions of gold from abroad; nor was this growth of bank reserves commensurate with the industrial and financial development of the country. Cash holdings of national banks, surplus reserves of New York clearing-house banks and money in circulation are indicative of a retardation in growth. Moreover, another important factor is to be found in a certain decentralization of reserves; which accompanied the increase in credit requirements. This does not mean that the practice of redepositing legal reserves in reserve and central reserve cities was discontinued, but that the greater demands for credit permitted less of the surplus funds to accumulate in those centers. This is partially indicated by the conservative growth of deposits and lawful money as shown in the statements of the New York banks during this period.

b. Banking capital and surplus as well as the number of banks formed was smaller in 1907 to 1912 than in the period 1902 to 1907:

	NUMBER OF		CAPITAL AND SURPLUS OF
	State Banks	*National Banks*	*National Banks*
1897	3,978	3,592	$879.7 million
1902	5,433	4,306	972.5 million
1907	9,334	6,306	1,407.0 million
1912	13,381	7,307	1,735.7 million

c. Banking efficiency made little progress. The drain upon bank reserves was heavy, for the inelastic bond-secured national-bank notes could not meet the growing need for money in circulation, nor could that need be met by the increased use of deposit currency. Furthermore, the absence of an organized discount market could not be offset by the small increase in interbank borrowing that occurred during this period.[1]

d. The heavy withdrawal of foreign capital, though the selling of securities, and the lessening of the supply of foreign loan funds, which brought also a restriction on American borrowing abroad, further limited the supply of bank credit.

Accumulation of savings seems to have proceeded at a rapid rate from 1908 to 1913:

[1] *Cf. Jour. of Pol. Econ.*, vol. xxix, p. 224, O. C. Lockhart, "Interbank Borrowing."

DEPOSITS IN SAVINGS BANKS IN U. S.

1890–99 = 100

1898 = 113	
1903 = 160	+ 47%
1908 = 200	+ 40%
1913 = 258	+ 58%

This accretion to the capital supply had several effects upon available bank credit:

a. Large capital accumulations demanded more credit, for purposes of coining purchasing power into means of payment.

b. Demands for capital were universally large, as shown in foregoing chapters, and the withdrawal of foreign capital from this country required replenishment by domestic capital, all of which involved an increased drain upon credit resources.

c. The employment of a part of domestic capital for this purpose naturally reduced the supply available for current business purposes and restricted the production of surplus commodities for foreign markets, by means of which gold imports might have been increased and bank reserves correspondingly augmented. However, the increased savings used to absorb securities, sold from abroad, served advantageously to prevent gold exports.

In addition to the influences above enumerated, the comparative trend of industrial and agricultural production seems to have exerted a decided influence in contracting the margin of credit elasticity.

Influence of Agricultural Production on the Elastic Credit Margin. There occurred, as we have seen, during this period 1907 to 1913, a striking divergence between the normal trends of mineral production and of manufacture, as compared with agricultural production:

PRODUCTION INDEX *

RELATIVE FIGURES WITH 1899 EQUALS 100

Years	Growth of population	Agriculture	Production of mining	Manufacturing
1899	100.0	100.0	100.0	100.0
1900	101.8	100.6	105.7	101.0
1901	103.8	89.3	114.6	112.4
1902	106.0	113.7	122.7	123.5
1903	108.1	105.0	135.0	125.5
1904	110.3	116.0	136.3	123.2
1905	112.4	117.5	161.6	144.4
1906	114.5	125.0	169.9	155.0
1907	116.7	112.4	185.9	156.3
1908	118.9	118.8	154.2	132.7
1909	121.0	118.1	189.4	163.4
1910	123.1	123.2	201.6	166.0
1911	125.3	117.0	194.4	158.3
1912	127.4	138.1	216.7	181.4
1913	129.6	122.1	227.2	187.1

* Index number of Mr. E. E. Day.

This disparity of development laid certain requirements upon the supply of credit, and, at the same time, forestalled possible accretions of gold for reserves as a basis for bank credit. The rapid development of industries required more capital and credit, while, on the other hand, the rapid rise in prices of foodstuffs and farm materials aided in perpetuating this increased demand.

A further aspect of this development may be seen in the fact that the expanding volume of industrial production was not accompanied by a corresponding growth in the domestic demand for these products, because of the retarded growth in the consuming power of the agricultural and transportation classes and of the commercial elements allied with the fortunes of these. This was due to the smaller agricultural production rather than to the prices ruling for agricultural commodities. The tendency toward persistent over-capitalization in industrial fields as a result of a continued in-

centive to business expansion, in the face of this depressing influence, required a readjustment. This readjustment involved the balancing or coordinating of production with demand. It could have been made in two ways:
first, through the domestic economic organization; or second, through foreign markets for the surplus industrial products. The former required that capitalization and capacity in the industrial fields be restricted in harmony with the retarded growth in demand caused by the underproduction in agriculture. This adjustment involved the elimination of the encroachment of cost prices of farm materials upon profits, which profits were also under pressure from the more slowly increasing selling prices of manufactured products and of the physical volume of business. The natural incentives to maintain capitalization by extension of credit were present,

Graph A

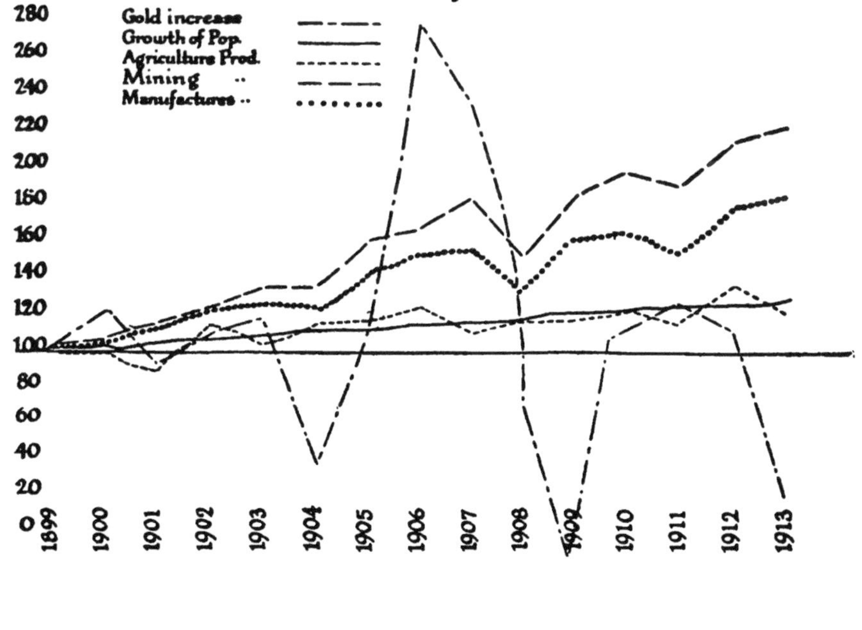

this credit being sought chiefly in the investment market. Of course, this could have been maintained until the slack in capacity and capitalization in the industrial fields had been absorbed by agricultural growth,, but time was not sufficient for this accomplishment during the period.

However, data of production and of imports of materials and foodstuffs as well as of exports of foodstuffs, materials and manufactures, for the United States, from 1908 to 1913, give evidence that business was seeking a permanent adjustment upon the basis of a continuance of the disparity between industrial and agricultural growth. The manner of this adjustment was by way partly of foreign trade. How incompletely the foreign markets offset the retarded growth in demand caused by the underproduction in agricultural development may be seen by the following data:

DATA ON IMPORTS AND EXPORTS OF THE UNITED STATES

RELATIVE FIGURES—1890–99 = 100

	Foodstuffs		*Raw Materials*		*Manufactures*	
Year	*Imports*	*Exports*	*Imports*	*Exports*	*Imports*	*Exports*
1908	112	124	196	194	174	311
1909	126	104	243	182	171	278
1910	125	88	395	197	215	318
1911	135	92	276	249	214	376
1912	163	100	300	252	215	423
1913	155	120	342	255	240	491
Average proportion over period to total imports and exports.	23.6%	22.6%	34.0%	32.3%	41.1%	44.5%

Analysis of table:

Net increase of exports of manufacture from 1908 to 1913, (gains in imports deducted from gains in exports) = 105%.

Net increase of imports of raw materials from 1908 to 1913, (gains in exports deducted from gains in imports) = 85%.

Net increase of imports of foodstuffs from 1908 to 1913, (gains in exports deducted from gains in imports) = 39%.

As indicated by these figures, the gain in foreign markets, though absorbing the rapidly growing volume of mineral and manufactured products, was, nevertheless, not sufficient to offset the effects of the retarded agricultural production. The greater requirements of capital and credit, to meet the higher costs of foodstuffs and farm materials and the importation of these commodities, as well as the expansion in production of minerals and manufactures, were not offset by an increase in capital and credit resources. The impossiblity of meeting, by a means of an increase in export of manufactures and miners products, the increase in imports of foodstuffs and materials, together with the retardation in growth of the exports of farm products and the withdrawal of foreign investments, led to a restriction upon gold imports. This conclusion is supported further by the fact that our favorable trade balance was considerably lessened in 1909 and 1910 but increased in 1911 to 1913. This increase, neverthelesss, was moderate in comparision with the industrial development from 1908 to 1913. Furthermore, this country was forced to meet the difficulties of a debtor nation.

Upon this analysis of the period 1908-1913, one may conclude that changes in the normal growth of agricultural production in relation to industrial development do exert an influence upon the supply of credit resources, and, therefore, upon the length of the business cycle. However, though the trend of agricultural production is a very important factor in the determination of the length of cycles, it represents only one of the many influences that contract or expand the margin of elasticity in the credit system.

Factors that Condition the Moment when Cycles Attain their Zenith and Nadir. Prosperity generally culminates when the limit of the expansibility of bank credit has been reached. The velocity at which this financial strain is developed, with its depressing influences upon business activity, may be determined by the following factors:

a. The extent and completeness of the business and price

readjustment in depression, this readjustment entailing the process of balancing of cost of selling prices and volume of business; the removal of disparity in price movements; the elimination of weak and inefficient concerns; and the liquidation of all debts, which seem unlikely to be paid off within reasonable periods of turnover of working capital for the various enterprises. The better this is accomplished, the sounder will be the basis for business expansion, and the sooner will revival occur.

b. The virility of business enterprise. This factor is the resultant of the multifarious forces that affect business profits. By and large, since the use of credit it such an important factor in the determination of business profits, the supply and price of bank credit, influenced though it is by the innumerable stimulating and depressing forces bombarding the business systems at all times, is the chief governor of business activity.

c. Proportionality of the distribution of funds obtained from banks and in the security markets. This is a highly significant factor, for the unequal flow of funds between the channels of incomes and expenditures, gives rise to lack of coordination between production and demand, and occasions, invariably, a disparity in price movements.

The moment when prices cease to decline and production attains its minimum, following the culmination of prosperity, may be forecast on the basis of the following conditions since each phase of the business cycle acquires its complexion from the forces generated in the preceding phases; therefore, the length and depth of depression may be gauged by:

1. The rapidity of the development of the financial strain in the preceding prosperity.

2. The disproportionate utilization of capital and credit resources accompanying business expansion, leading to the unequal flow of incomes and expenditures.

3. The resultant disparity of capitalizations among business enterprises, or among fields of industry.

4. The extent and dissimilitude of overstocks of current goods and of construction arising therefrom.

5. The concomitant disarrangements in the movements of prices.

The greater the extent to which the above conditions have developed, the more prolonged and difficult will be the ensuing liquidation and readjustments.

6. The supply of bank credit remaining available and the nature of the banking policy in regulating liquidation. The channels of income and outgo become smaller because of unemployment, lessening profits and contraction in the purchases of business enterprises. Second, the volume of funds in circulation becomes smaller, (a.) through hoarding, and, later in the liquidation process, through lack of investment opportunities at a profit, and (b.) through the crystallization of funds into frozen credits as a result of unmarketable merchandise and collateral, and the non-collectibility of receivables. Not only therefore, is the quantity of funds in circulation diminished, but also the rate of flow is reduced. Third, flow of funds resolves itself largely into the work of liquidating debts—the offsetting of debits,—rather than into the work of exchanging goods. For the time being, the work of reducing reducible debts takes precedence. As a result of the immobility of assets and the necessity of meeting pressing obligations, there always occurs during the immediate period, after liquidation has begun, an expansion of bank loans. Any banking policy that is not coordinated or competitive and lenient in granting and renewing loans, both with respect to the amount and discount rate,—provided a panic has been avoided,—will prolong the liquidation process since the tendency to hold commodities for higher prices becomes common in such periods.

Corroboration of above Principles in 1908-10 and 1911-13. Panic conditions afford rapid adjustments, by forcing losses. Panics are caused by the absolute limitation on means of payment which suddenly halts business activity, concomitant with a sudden drop in prices and cessation of production. The character of the adjustment, —as shown in Chapter I—during the latter part of 1907 and first part of 1908, demonstrated its incompleteness. The time was too short for a complete overhauling of the business system. The early and extraordinary rise of speculative activity, and the disproportionate use of the abundant supply of cheap funds were responsible for the premature culmination of a vigorous revival and for an unsound and abortive prosperity, in the beginning of 1910. The serious maladjustments present in the production and price systems required all of 1910 and most of 1911 for correction. Moreover, the liquidation process was carried on under a prolonged financial strain throughout 1910, due to the drain upon our credit resources, as previously explained.[1] All of this laid the basis for the long depression, although the continuance of prosperity abroad buoyed up business conditions in this country, during 1910-11, and counteracted an otherwise serious state of depression.

Again, the prolonged moderate depression in 1910 and 1911 gave ample opportunity for production and price adjustments, so that the prosperity period of 1912 was ushered in upon a sound basis. The supply and price of credit was only moderate, thus restricting undue speculation incentives. The subsequent development of business activity was well balanced, and, leaving no heritage of serious maladjustments, brought about the smooth, short and easy recession of 1913. It must be observed, however, that business liqui-

[1] *Cf. supra*, chap. iii.

dation abroad and in this country, did not run its true course, because of political complications and apprehensions of war. These political complications and their influence upon economic factors were the chief characteristics of the period 1908 to 1913.

The foregoing analysis, based upon our study of the period 1908 to 1913, seems to indicate the following conclusions:

a. That the limits of elasticity in the credit system, defined on the one hand by the minimum of credit requirements in depressions, and, on the other, by the amount of bank reserves regulate the spurts in prices and production, namely, the lengths of the business cycles herein examined.

b. That the relation between the normal trend of agricultural production and industrial development during this period was one of the several important factors which affected the relatively permanent requirements of credit, and the supply of bank reserves.

c. That the moment when the two cycles of 1908 to 1911 and 1911 to 1913 attained their zenith and their nadir was determined chiefly by the supply of bank credit and the use made of it.

Bei Fragen zur Produktsicherheit wenden Sie sich bitte an:
If you have any questions regarding product safety,
please contact:

Walter de Gruyter GmbH
Genthiner Straße 13
10785 Berlin
productsafety@degruyterbrill.com